WHAT PEOPLE A

MW01038518

COLLISION WITH JOY

"I highly recommend *Collision With Joy*! As a pastor, author and seminary professor, I have read many books on grief and many others on Heaven. Melody combines the best of all of them in one book. As she writes about her own pain as a mom who lost her daughter to a tragic car accident, the reader is led to feel Melody's gnawing ache, her questions and the heavenly perspective that was her source of comfort through her grieving process.

"The truly unique aspect of Melody's book lay in her vivid descriptions of what she imagines her daughter was experiencing in Heaven while she was grieving as a mom on Earth. I found Melody's picture of Heaven to be theologically accurate, wonderfully creative and very reassuring. I have not suffered the loss of a close relative, but I still became excited thinking about the prospect of Heaven in ways that I normally do not. By the end of the book, it was easy to see why Melody's effort to look at suffering in light of eternity served her so well in processing her own grief.

"*Collision With Joy* is a book that will appeal to anyone who longs to see a practical reason why the anticipation of what awaits believers in Heaven can be such an amazing comfort here on earth."

Dr. George Kenworthy, Founder/CEO of Hope for the Hurting Home and author of *Before the Last Resort*

"Melody Richards is personally acquainted with grief but she is also intimately acquainted with the Lord Jesus Christ. You will be lovingly counseled and deeply consoled as you journey with her through the death of her daughter. The reality of Heaven will come through in living color as she envisions her daughter in the presence of Jesus. But then you will be brought back to earth, back to the sorrow of a mother's heart, to see the very real comfort the Lord provides and the transforming power of living with a great hope."

Charles Morris, President of Haven Ministries, and Janet Morris, authors of *Saving a Life* and *Jesus in the Midst of Success*.

"Melody Richards paints a picture of loss that includes both pain and victory. Melody sees the whole picture because she has eternity in view, not just the now. Her book is a life-changer."

Jan Markell, Founder, President of Olive Tree Ministries and Host of Understanding the Times

"One of the worst losses there is occurs when a mother loses a child. Melody describes the loss, exploring the devastation and plumbing the depths of her emotions. But she does more than that. Her book also provides instruction and hope. I was especially intrigued by how she finds hope. Throughout the book she takes short visits to Heaven, imaging her sweet daughter, Danielle, experiencing the bliss and peace and comfort of finally being home. That home empowered Melody to make her home in a world of suffering and pain. Hope indeed! I was moved by her account. I trust readers will be, too."

Jerry Sittser, Professor of Theology and author of *A Grace Disguised* and *A Grace Revealed*

COLLISION
with JOY

GLIMPSES *of* HEAVEN IN THE MIDST *of* LOSS

MELODY RICHARDS

IN LOVING MEMORY OF DANIELLE

Dedicated to Ashley and Nathan

I am incredibly blessed to have you as my children—such
treasures in my life! I am excited about the day we are
all reunited with Danielle for a joy-filled eternity together.
I love you, Mom

A NOTE FROM MELODY

⊸⊶

I t has been five years since my precious daughter, Danielle, was killed in a car accident and ushered into the arms of Jesus. My journey through grief has become an opportunity for God to show me hope and joy in ways I never imagined would be possible.

My goal in writing *Collision with Joy* is to provide hope. I write from the perspective of a grieving mom as well as a professional counselor. Much of the material I will share with you comes from three years of daily journaling through the brokenness and healing. Although there were many aspects that contributed to my healing, developing an excitement and passion for Heaven has been instrumental. When I truly embraced the truth that Heaven was my home, I began to develop an *eternal perspective* that understands all sorrow is temporary. It is my prayer that this truth will grab your heart and give you hope.

Collision with Joy uses complementary storylines alternating between my personal reflections on the difficult questions of loss and *fictional* scenes depicting Danielle's dramatic and beautiful welcome to her eternal home. The transition to the fictional heavenly scenes will be portrayed through a different font. It is my heartfelt desire that pulling back the curtain (so to speak) and imagining the cosmic drama through fictional scenes from Heaven, will touch your emotions and inspire your mind in an unforgettable way. All of the events and dialogues that occur in the heavenly scenes are my attempt to portray Heaven in a way that conforms to—or at least does not violate any Biblical truth.

Developing an eternal perspective gives us a reason to continue, no matter what kinds of hardships we encounter. Living with eternity in mind transforms the way we view loss or suffering. I'm praying this book will minister to anyone who needs a renewed, Biblical vision of Heaven.

As you read, I hope you, too, will experience a growing excitement and passion for all that Heaven holds. May we remain unsurprised by the trials, disappointments, and black nights of grief in this world, but amazed and renewed by the joy set before us for the next.

You are profoundly loved.

CONTENTS

Chapter One:

NO ORDINARY NIGHT

———∞∞∞———

F riday, May 16, 2008 came to a close like a foretaste of Heaven. I went to bed feeling extremely blessed as I reflected on the day.

Earlier that afternoon, I had a delightful conversation with Danielle. She had just completed her last exam at Bethel University and called me, feeling simply ecstatic. I had also spoken to Ashley, my seventeen-year-old daughter, a few hours earlier. She, too, was on an emotional high after recently being accepted into a program where she would be spending her final year of high school at Bethel University with Danielle. I had just tucked in my basketball-loving son Nathan. At eleven years old, his frequent hugs and enthusiastic conversations filled me with joy.

Feeling content as I snuggled into bed, I glanced over to the nightstand and smiled as I picked up Danielle's two-page Mother's Day letter written just five days earlier. I re-read it, as I had every night that week, savoring every word Danielle had used to express her love for me. I picked up a couple of the coupons she had included in the letter: coupons for dinner dates, lunch dates, rollerblading, and tennis. My eyes welled with tears recalling the precious moment she gave me the card and an emotional hug. I made a mental note to call Danielle in the morning and schedule a date to use one of the lunch coupons. The moment was tranquil and beautiful as I lay cuddled in the memories.

I sat bolt upright and wondered for a moment where I was. There was a loud knock as someone rapped on the front door again. My mind raced and immediately I thought it had to be Ashley. She must have decided to come home early from her sleepover. I hoped everything was okay and she wasn't sick. I walked downstairs to let her in.

As I approached the front door, I froze. A nearby street lamp cast a glow across the porch, silhouetting the unmistakable form of a police officer. Instantly, panic surged through my body. My hand refused to open the door. The officer knocked again and jolted me out of denial. I reached for the handle, opened the door in slow motion, and gestured for him to come in. He must have seen the terror in my eyes as he walked in. A mother's worst nightmare came slamming into reality as he assumed his seasoned, official voice.

"I'm so sorry to tell you. Danielle was in a car accident and she did not survive."

I collapsed and laid there in a heap, convulsing as anguish coursed through my being. I don't recall my conversation with the officer. Somehow, I eventually dragged myself upstairs, then crumpled into a sobbing heap in the corner of the bedroom. Darkness and despair completely enveloped me and I remember doubting this was a journey I could survive. I wanted to die so the pain would stop and I could just be with my precious Danielle.

As I lay there crying in the dark, I found only one shred of comfort—the assurance that after Danielle took her last breath in the wreckage of her car, she immediately went Home to Jesus. I had this hope because Danielle trusted in Jesus as her Lord and Savior.

While I was curled up in the corner, my senses were suddenly suffused with a soft light. My eyes were closed but the glow was in total contrast to the complete darkness in my bedroom and soul. Unexpectedly, a warmth began to wash over me and I saw the picture. Jesus was tenderly embracing my darling Danielle. The soft light slowly grew more radiant as I realized the two of them were its focal point. An unexplainable comfort surged over me as I clung to this vivid reminder that my precious daughter was now Home with her beloved Lord.

I am not sure how long the vision lasted, but it is a memory that is forever etched into my mind. To be given this privilege of seeing Danielle in the arms of Jesus, knowing that she was eternally safe, was a place of refuge from the pain to come.

The rest of the night was torturous—a blur of panic and overwhelming grief interspersed with erratic thoughts that this must be a nightmare. Waves of nausea crashed over me as I lay weeping and crying out to God for help, having neither the strength nor the will to even move.

Eventually maternal instincts kicked in and I knew I had to tell Ashley and Nathan. In addition to the emotional agony that had now settled in and become a part of me, intense fear threatened to overwhelm me. I scrambled to find the best way to communicate this horrific tragedy to Danielle's brother and sister. It seemed so unfair that they had to deal with this shocking reality at such young ages. I wondered if they would ever bounce back from this emotional trauma. Ashley was due home from her sleepover by 6:00 AM to make an early morning soccer practice, so I decided to wait to share the dreadful news with her then.

The emotions I experienced as I sat at the kitchen table are difficult to describe. One that stands out is the numbness. I felt a sense of dread waiting for Ashley and concerned about how she would react, yet at the same time it felt as if my feelings had switched off. I tried to pray, not even sure what to pray for, but knowing that God understood my anguish.

My heart raced and my head swam as I heard the back door open. The time had come too quickly and I wasn't prepared. Ashley walked into the house and reared back when she saw my tears and disheveled state. I stood up and put my arms around her and echoed the officer's announcement, "Danielle has been in an accident...and she did not survive," adding, "she's with Jesus."

She started screaming hysterically, "No! No! No! *Not* Danielle!"

It almost wrenched my soul out of my body to see my daughter having to experience what I went through just hours before. I just held her as she screamed and wrestled with the horror of instantly losing her sister and best friend.

Nathan came dashing into the kitchen. I turned to look at him and saw the horrible look of fright in his eyes. I released Ashley and rushed over to Nathan and hugged him. Tears flooded his face as I shared the overwhelming news about his sister one more time. Though he remained silent, the horror in his expression told me his feelings. I added the comforting truth that Danielle was with Jesus, but he just walked to the living room in shock. For the next hour he did not move from the window where he simply stared with rivers streaming down his cheeks. I longed to protect him from this pain but, of course, that was impossible.

In a single moment, the family we had cherished was changed forever. We had been plunged into a new reality that terrified us—an existence without Danielle that would impact the rest of our lives. Would there, ever again, be a waking moment not filled with agony?

After talking to Ashley and Nathan, I began the emotionally arduous task of contacting family and friends. I called my brothers first and we sobbed together over the phone. I sensed the doubling of their sorrow as they absorbed the loss of their niece while feeling my pain too.

I knew I had to tell my mom in person. Just nine months earlier, she lost her beloved husband of almost fifty years. As I drove over to her house with my brother, I thought: *I lost my dad. Now my daughter. This has to be a nightmare and I'll soon wake up.* I had often said, "I can handle just about anything, but not the death of any of my children.*"*

When we walked in, Mom was still in her robe, at the kitchen table, reading her Bible. She looked up, excited to see us, but her expression quickly changed as she saw my tear-filled eyes. We told her the awful news and the anguish in her face tore my heart open afresh.

I went home and managed to call a few more friends, but soon was too drained to tell the story again. As I spoke with different people, I could distinguish the unique tones of their horror over the phone as they heard the dreadful news. My anxiety mounted with each of those calls.

Later that morning, Ashley drove over to Bethel University to tell Danielle's friends in person. When she arrived back home that evening, she shared through tears the deep agony of Danielle's friends when hearing the news. Some literally dropped to the ground, while others just started screaming. A ripple of sadness quickly spread through the campus as more and more students were told about Danielle. Within an hour, there were clusters of students throughout the campus crying, praying, and sharing "Danielle stories." It became evident just how uniquely special Danielle had made people feel.

Friends and family began to fill our home. Every person who walked through the door brought a fresh flood of tears. People arrived in waves to support us, love us, and pray with us. They brought food, beverages, flowers, and willing hands to do whatever was needed. Most importantly, they brought their love, compassionate hearts, hugs, and tears.

In the early evening, Ashley and a few of Danielle's friends from Bethel showed up. They had packed up all of her belongings from the dorm and carried the boxes into her room at home. Their red, swollen eyes said it all. As we hugged, some would shake while others felt like limp rag dolls. After they left, I went into Danielle's room, fell on her bed and just wept. As I clutched some of her stuffed animals, my glance moved to the dresser. Seeing her framed baby picture released another flood of emotions as I recalled the day of her birth, holding her and feeling such intense love.

I sobbed, "Oh Lord, she's so young. She had her whole life ahead of her. Why did this happen?"

I was still stunned from the incredible noise of the impact. My car was deathly still. A really tall man with the kindest face approached my window and looked in. Something about him was so familiar. He seemed like a close friend that I just couldn't place. Strange. He leaned into the car and lifted me as gently as though his hands were made of lambswool. I wondered how he would maneuver me through the mangled window.

Suddenly we were hovering above the highway as I lay comfortably in his arms. I looked over at the car and stared for a second, confused. My broken body was still in the driver's seat. I turned and looked up at my friend. He tilted his head ever so slightly, blinked and gave a tiny nod that as if to say, *It's all going to be okay.* I felt compassion emanating from his entire being as he held me like I was a feather. I looked back at the scene. My body left in the car seemed so pitiful and weak in contrast to the strength and delight I was experiencing in the man's arms.

In an instant, another man appeared. I realized both men had a slight glow radiating from them. I was mesmerized. The two men shared a nod of affirmation. I looked up to see what they were agreeing to as clouds suddenly rushed toward my face. This was absolutely awesome! A sense of peace washed over me.

With impossible speed we rocketed past planets, stars, galaxies and unspeakable wonders. Then it hit me. Jesus! I was about to see my Lord, face to face. In a way I can't explain, my escorts sensed my realization and as if synchronized, both turned to me, beaming with joy. I looked up at my friend carrying me and the smile in his eyes said it all: *Yes, you're about to meet the King.*

Chapter Two:

THE PAIN OF PREPARATION

―◦◦◦―

That night, after I had hugged and thanked the last friend for the day, I closed the front door and just stood there for a minute, wrestling again with the horrible reality of our traumatized home. I dragged myself to Danielle's room and turned on the light. Her boxes were in the corner filled with books, supplies, and clothes. Things she had been using and wearing just a day ago. It was beyond surreal. I grabbed a couple of Danielle's stuffed animals, fell on her bed, and sobbed inconsolably.

After a few minutes, I sighed and looked over to see that Danielle's Bible had been placed on her dresser. I reached over and turned to Revelation 21:4, which she had underlined. "He will wipe every tear from their eyes. There will be no more death or mourning or crying or pain, for the old order of things has passed away."

Tears filled my eyes again. "Oh God!" I wept. "I know she will never face pain, nor will she cry again...but will the tears ever stop for me?" My thoughts began tormenting me. "Will our family survive this crisis thrust upon us with no warning?" Fear's icy fingers began to grip my heart. All my hopes and dreams of Danielle graduating from college, getting married, having children and living a full and meaningful life were suddenly shattered. The emptiness I felt as

I reflected on the loss was overwhelming. I knew I would never fall asleep with these thoughts swirling in my mind, so I got up and started reading some verses that a friend had put together for me.

Isaiah 41:10 especially strengthened me at that time: "So do not fear, for I am with you; do not be dismayed, for I am your God. I will strengthen you and help you; I will uphold you with my righteous right hand." I began begging God to strengthen me, help me and hold me. Then I read a verse I hadn't noticed before. Isaiah 45:3 says, "I will give you hidden treasures, riches stored in secret places, so that you may know that I am the LORD, the God of Israel, who summons you by name."

As I read that verse for a second time, my thoughts went back to almost twenty four hours earlier. God had sent me a treasure in the middle of the night as I lay in the darkness of my bedroom, utterly consumed by grief: the image of Jesus holding Danielle. I reflected on the verse I had just read, realizing God had given me this gift so I would know that even though He is Lord of all, He cares about me personally. I felt God comforting me, reminding me again that Danielle was safely home. It was in this moment I asked God to help me to see this tragedy through His eyes—from an eternal perspective. Eventually, exhausted by grief, I fell asleep.

In an instant we soared past stars, nebulae and galaxies. My mind was comprehending wonders that I knew could only be spiritually fathomed. Although the trip seemed like hours, and at the same time a mere moment, we were suddenly standing before a gigantic gate. The powerful man gently set me on my feet and smiled. I looked up at the massive, towering gates that shimmered with a satin sheen that refracted a myriad of brilliant colors. As I thought that they resembled a mother-of-pearl ring I had, a reference I'd heard in a few worship songs suddenly made sense. These were the gates of pearl. I trembled as I took a step forward.

As if on cue, the gates slowly opened for me without so much a squeak. In the distance was a bright, yet suffused, soft light that was without a doubt drawing me toward it. It grew brighter as I walked past the gates, mesmerized. As I walked, I noticed some figures approaching from the direction of that great light.

Something in my spirit surged. I had never felt such an indescribable peace as I drew closer to the light. I then realized there was a small crowd, silhouetted by the great light. Suddenly I squealed with joy as I recognized three, very distinct faces. My grandparents had all come to welcome me and were equally overjoyed. I ran over and flung my arms around each of them. With beaming smiles, they each embraced me and welcomed me home. I was so excited to see them, it took me a minute to realize there were even more friends and family members gathered around me. Everyone was filled with joy. Many hands clasped my own as loved ones swarmed around me, some of whom I hadn't met on earth but somehow knew intuitively who they were. Everyone radiated such intense joy, excitement and warmth that I had never experienced before. I sighed deeply as I took it all in—the youthful yet wise faces around me, the immense beauty of this place and the pure magnificence of the entire scene. It felt like a dream. But I knew this was more real than my life on earth had ever been.

It finally dawned on me that the source of the light was at the back of the crowd, emanating the pure joy and peace that was engulfing us all. A figure stood out somehow, glowing with the soft light that drew and captivated my eyes. I saw the others deferring to the figure, who grew clearer in the light, and they all stepped aside. I took a step forward, my eyes wide with awe, knowing in my heart who this was. A kind, beautiful, bearded face, full of pure love and what can only be described as contagious joy, smiled tenderly at me. Trembling, I tilted my head up and exhaled in exhilaration at the immediate and tremendous realization of who it was. My beloved Lord Jesus stepped forward and took my fragile hand in His own. With the very hand that had spun the universe into being, Jesus pulled me into His arms and squeezed me tightly.

"Welcome, Danielle, my precious daughter!" He whispered just to me. "I can't wait for you to see the kingdom I've prepared for you." With a smile that communicated more than any I had ever seen, Jesus looked into my eyes and said with immense pride, "Well done, my good and faithful servant. Enter into the joy of your Lord!"

The crowd erupted in cheers.

Overwhelmed by the majesty and holiness of my Lord, I suddenly dropped face-down to the ground before Him. I felt Him kneel gently and raised me by the arm. "You can rise, my daughter. You have transitioned from mortality to life. This is your eternal home, which I've made for you to enjoy with Me."

I looked up, and as I gazed deeply into His eyes, transfixed by purity and love, I felt a big bump on His palm. I looked down and saw the deep and ugly scar. It was quite the contrast from the perfection and wonder reflected by the rest of Him. I looked at Him, knowing what the scar was but questioning why He still bore it. Without a word, He communicated that the scar too was perfection. He had perfectly finished His work of redemption for me and the scar bore testimony of His love and the sacrifice He'd made so I could be here with Him.

I threw my arms around my Savior's neck and hugged Him tighter than anyone I'd ever hugged before. Instead of protesting, He laughed deeply and heartily and then cried, "Danielle! You've entered into the joy of your Lord!"

The crowd burst out into a cheer again and I was sure the celebration could be heard for miles around.[1]

The next morning, I awoke, looked around, and thought, *What a terrifying nightmare.* I walked downstairs and my heart sank as I saw the flowers that friends and family had brought the day before—a vivid reminder that the nightmare was real. The tears started streaming down my cheeks again as I collapsed into the kitchen chair. I felt truly frightened and so alone. My Bible was on the table and I reached for it, praying for any comfort I could get. I thought I was dependent on Jesus before, but I had no clue how dependent I would become. I went to one of my favorite verses:

> Do you not know? Have you not heard? The LORD is the everlasting God, the Creator of the ends of the earth. He will not grow tired or weary, and his understanding no one can fathom. He gives strength to the weary and increases the power of the weak. Even youths grow tired and weary, and young men stumble and fall; but those who hope in the LORD will renew their strength. They will soar on wings like eagles; they will run and not grow weary, they will walk and not be faint. (Isaiah 40:28-31)

As I read this passage, I realized I had absolutely nowhere to turn but to my Lord and Savior. I desperately needed to release to Him the anguish that was crushing my heart. I needed God's strength and power to make it through this journey. I struggled with how to do this as my mind filled with the emotional tasks that all parents who lose children have to face.

Never in my worst nightmare would I have ever imagined myself sitting at the computer, writing Danielle's memorial bulletin and her obituary for the local newspaper. She was only twenty years old. Her life was just beginning. I could barely see the computer, my eyes were so clouded with tears. What could I say with words that could possibly encapsulate the joy and energy of our Danielle?

The next dreaded decision was choosing an outfit for Danielle. As I sat there in tears, staring at her clothes in the closet, I thought of the many times I had chosen clothing for

Danielle. Which cute, frilly dress should she wear for her first birthday? Her first day of kindergarten? Even more recently, I had helped to pick out her homecoming dress and prom dress. Just a few months earlier she called me from Bethel and asked if I could bring over one of her old prom dresses because she was going to the Bethel banquet that night. She and I laughed on the phone as I was searching the closet, describing the various dress options for her. There was no laughter today as I went through her closet. The contrast felt cruel and stark as I was overwhelmed with emotion. I began crying and thought, *I can't do this.*

I went downstairs, and when I checked my computer, someone had just emailed me a note of encouragement with verses from Psalm 30. I read the entire passage, which was about crying out to the Lord for help. Verse 11 caught my attention at that moment: "You turned my wailing into dancing; you removed my sackcloth and clothed me with joy."

A sense of hope began returning as I reflected on this promise. Yes, I was feeling intense pain selecting physical clothing in which to lay Danielle's body to rest. Yet God promised to *clothe* me with *joy*. I did not think for one second that the timing of that email was coincidental. Instead, I knew God was using a friend to encourage me.

Three videos were created for the visitation and during the funeral. Picking out photographs for the video and poster boards elicited another surge of emotions within me. Two years earlier, I had created a number of poster boards for Danielle's graduation party. I remember sitting there with her, laughing over some of the pictures of her childhood and mission trips, and reminiscing over the memories they rekindled. It was a special time for us as we shared stories while we selected pictures, joking about which photos were going to be used for her wedding video.

Now, instead of creating a wedding video, we were creating a funeral video, and the depth of pain was simply unbearable. It also brought back memories from nine months earlier when my mom and brothers sat around our kitchen table with me, going through pictures to be used at my dad's funeral. We had been looking through pictures spanning a lifetime of eighty years, while I was now creating a story with pictures bridging a twenty-year span. As I sat there, tearfully sorting through memories of Danielle and the photos that sparked these to life once more, I remember desperately wishing to glimpse how happy my beautiful daughter was in Heaven.

Sick with grief and exhausted from the unrelenting agony, I sat staring at my daughter's computer screen. With every new file I found, Danielle seemed to leap off the page. Her vibrant passion for life and beautiful, giving nature were etched into even the most mundane trivia. It was well past midnight and I knew I desperately needed to sleep but I couldn't tear myself away. As I continued scanning through the files, one was titled, *Testimony*. A surge of emotion rippled through me:

> Growing up in a Christian home, I accepted Christ into my life at the age of five. After gaining more knowledge over the years, I recommitted my life to Christ at the age of sixteen. I attended Heritage Christian Academy through 8th grade and graduated from Armstrong High School. Through the years I experienced many joys and also faced hardships. These experiences have shaped who I have become. God has always been there for me, even when I struggled.
>
> In high school I went on four mission trips to Mexico, Colorado, Nicaragua, and Kansas City. These experiences were life-changing for me as I saw God answer so many prayers. These

experiences impacted me so much that I have considered going into the mission field.

As a student at Bethel University, I am pursuing a degree in psychology and hope to eventually receive a master's degree. I am interested in a career that involves helping others. I am attending a Christian college to help me continue to grow closer to God. My desire is to represent God's love to others on a daily basis.

As I read this testimony, tears streamed down my face again. Although heart-wrenching, it was also comforting and a source of hope. I pondered this small hope piercing through the agony. As I meditated on the astounding assurance of victory over death, a peace descended upon me. As I headed for bed, one specific phrase just kept surfacing in my thoughts over and over again. *Danielle is home.*

I knew it was the Holy Spirit's voice as my mind and heart wrapped around those words. I drifted off to sleep, repeating them over and over: *Danielle is home. Danielle is home. Danielle is home.*

Chapter Three:

CELEBRATING DANIELLE'S LIFE

—∞∞—

T he next day, reality fully solidified itself as we continued to deal with the inevitable funeral arrangements. My two main requests were that Danielle's funeral would glorify God and that it would focus on celebrating her home-going rather than lament her leaving us.

As the day of the funeral drew closer, I knew I would soon have to face the culminating reality of seeing Danielle's body, and I wasn't sure how I would handle it. Sleep was impossible, so I walked outside and sat on our deck. I sat there in the darkness crying out to Jesus to remove some of the anguish, even for a moment of relief. I looked over to the house and noticed I had left a few lights on. Seeing the glowing lights against the inky darkness made me think of Matthew 5:14: "You are the light of the world. A town built on a hill cannot be hidden."

It was a powerful picture of what I wanted to see at the funeral. I knew there would be people attending who saw only the darkness and had no hope of ever seeing their precious friend Danielle again. I wanted Christ to be that Light and for Him to shine brightly that day. I asked God to give me strength to be the light He called me to be. I longed for the funeral to illuminate the darkness for those who had no hope.

As loved ones thronged around us, I had a thousand questions to ask my Lord. Like an ultra-perceptive best friend, He just looked at me knowingly and gave me the warmest smile. "We'll have plenty of time for all the answers. I just want to celebrate with you for this moment."

In a rush of pure, swooning love, I knew I would do absolutely anything for my magnificent, yet entirely approachable Lord.

"Let's walk," He said, motioning with His head. "I have a lot to show you, Danielle." He took my hand again and I could feel the peaking excitement of my friends and family. Everything, and I mean absolutely *everything*, was just overflowing with life and joy. As we turned, I noticed a majestic range of mountains in the distance, capped with story book snow. I had somehow not seen them until now. Jesus smiled again with eyes that couldn't hide His joy if they tried, and He led me in the direction of the mountains. Again I felt that rush of pure joy and exhilaration.

I realized I was walking barefoot on the softest grass I'd ever felt, and I saw the most gorgeous fruit trees to my right and left. In the distance, I was sure I could hear the faint gurgle of a river. Everything was full of life. I looked at a tree almost directly in front of me and saw the brightest, most delicious-looking fruit I'd ever seen, but I just kept walking. I wasn't sure if I could have any of the fruit. As we passed the next group of trees, Jesus, knowing my desire, took me over to a tree that was heavy with even more delectable fruit. He picked the biggest piece off a branch and nonchalantly tossed it over to me. I caught it and looked at Him slightly surprised.

"Have a bite!" He said with a grin.

I bit into the golden-red skin of the fruit that looked like a cross between an apple and a mango, but only shinier and more...glowy? My eyes widened as the most delicious mix of sweet and just slightly tart fruit and juice filled my mouth.

"Oh wow!" I mumbled through chipmunk cheeks.

"Hahaha!" He bellowed, as did everyone around me.

Not only was the fruit the most delicious thing I had ever eaten, as it filled my mouth and I swallowed, it radiated life and energy into my body. Jesus chuckled again as He watched my reactions while biting off an even bigger piece.

For a moment I paused and looked at Jesus, whose expression softened in compassion. "What about my family, Lord?"

He ran His hand over my head and said, in a way that carried the secure assurance of a father, "I promise you I will comfort them, Danielle. They cannot understand your joy right now, but in time they will know you are safe and in a far better place."

I thought of my family and how devastated they had to be. I thought about other loved ones. It had to be an unthinkably difficult time for them. If only I could tell them how happy I was.

I felt Jesus put His strong yet gentle arm around me again as I stared ahead, wondering how my family was doing.

He softly said, "I have them in the palm of My hand, Danielle. They will make it through their loss stronger than ever. I will show them your joy in the safety of your eternal home. Remember, I am the balm of Gilead."

I remembered the balm of Gilead. Now I understood more than ever before that Jesus is that precious, healing, spiritual ointment—the One who can cure any ailment and bring wholeness to any torn heart. Immediately, I felt relief. I was utterly confident that my Lord would fulfill His promise to me. He took my shoulders tenderly in His hands and, with deep compassion, looked into my eyes again with utmost reassurance. I smiled at Him in total adoration for a few seconds.

I then peered past Him and pointed. "Can we go see those?"

He turned and looked at the grand mountains I was pointing to. Another huge smile broke out across His face and He said, "Of course, My precious child! I knew you'd love those...but first I have something else to show you."

The evening of Danielle's visitation arrived and I took a deep breath as I looked at myself in the mirror. I had managed to get dressed and appeared ready to attend the visitation. *You can do this*, I told myself, and anxiously tried to believe it. I gathered up the family and we trudged to the car.

I was told later that the evening of the visitation was perfectly warm and presented an unusually beautiful sunset. I didn't notice anything. I walked into our church and looked around in awe. My loving friends had done a breath-taking job of creating a picturesque setting. The tables were strewn with pink flower petals, pink feathers, and decorated with family pictures. It truly created an atmosphere filled with loving memories of Danielle. Along the windows of the church foyer were the poster boards we had created and six more her friends had made. I dabbed at the fresh welling of tears as I looked around.

My attention was drawn to a large room off to the side where I could see her coffin. I thought, *I can't do this, I cannot bear to see my daughter lying in a coffin. Oh God, please help me.* As I continued to walk toward the coffin, I felt an overwhelming sense of dread and anguish. By the time I reached Danielle, the tears were flowing again and I had started to shake. My hand shook uncontrollably as I caressed her face. I reached down and gave her a hug, feeling such profound sadness because for the first time ever, she didn't hug me back. As I stood there caressing her hands, I kept reminding myself, *This is not Danielle, this is just her empty body. She's with Jesus.* Trembling, I leaned over and kissed her forehead.

I staggered away from the coffin and was quickly surrounded by friends and family. I noticed many of Danielle's friends were also there, and they seemed to desperately need comfort. I knew they needed to see God's light shining through this tragedy. Despite being heavily laden with grief, I felt God lavishing His grace upon me, giving me the ability to reach out to others. There were so many people praying for our family, and I could feel these prayers being transformed by God into the strength and compassion that I needed at that time.

I looked around again and was really amazed at the number of students and young adults present. Most were visibly grief-stricken, and as I stood looking at this group of brokenhearted young people, I was suddenly overwhelmed with a sensation of hope that carried with it this thought: *These are Danielle's friends and I want to reach every one of them for Jesus.* I prayed that God would give me or someone else an opportunity to share His love with them.

After reminiscing for a while, we all took our seats and began a time of sharing. The memories of Danielle were comforting, yet extraordinarily emotional. I felt so much gratitude that so many had come to offer their love and support in testimony of how Danielle had brought joy to others. It was abundantly clear from everyone's fond memories of Danielle that she had loved life, loved people, and loved to have fun. Many stories illustrated her playful, fun-loving spirit. One in particular perfectly captured Danielle's desire to make the best of any circumstance. She and her friend were at a cabin and had planned to go jet-skiing. It turned out to be cold and rainy and most people would have allowed this miserable weather to ruin their attitude and their fun, but never Danielle. The girls put on their warmest clothes and jackets, covered it all with clean garbage bags and sealed these with Saran Wrap. They then proceeded to have the time of their life jet-skiing on the lake, fully clothed, in the rain.

It was evident, too, how much Danielle genuinely cared about people. She was incredibly compassionate and loved to encourage people. I was overwhelmed at how many stories depicting these character traits were told during our time of sharing. One story that exemplified Danielle's heart was shared by one of her friends.

> Danielle was a model of compassion and generosity. I remember in youth group when I just started to come, she would always be so welcoming. She is

the kind of person you love to be around. She was always positive and full of joy. She also had a love for Jesus and enjoyed talking about what God was doing in her life and how she wanted to live for Him. Oh, how I miss Danielle.

As I listened to her friends sharing about how Danielle had impacted their life in some way, I realized there might be friends who did not have a relationship with Jesus. Reflecting on the powerful emotions I had experienced earlier, I ached to share God's love with them. However, I began to think this desire didn't make sense. I had no way of reaching these young adults. Little did I know, God always finds a way of converting His desire into reality. I had no way of knowing that though, outside of pure faith, and unfortunately that night I was left with little as I walked out of the church, emotionally and physically drained.

––––––

The morning of the funeral arrived far too quickly. As if in agreement with Danielle's sunny, cloudless attitude toward life, the day was absolutely gorgeous. As we got dressed and ready to go to the church, I found myself fighting the finality of it. Frantically, I wondered again whether I'd have the strength to face this day. I took a deep breath and asked God for comfort and strength.

Right before the funeral service, our family had a final opportunity to view the open casket. One by one, family members slowly said their final goodbyes. I remember gripping the side of the casket. My shaking legs were struggling to hold me up as I gazed at Danielle's beautiful face one last time. It was a heartbreaking moment, hugging Danielle for the final time on this side of Heaven.

After we took our seats and were welcomed by the pastor, a friend with a beautiful voice sang, "I Can Only Imagine" by Mercy Me. The uplifting lyrics, painting a picture of seeing Jesus in Heaven, were comforting yet emotional, as we grasped the truth that Danielle was actually in Heaven with Jesus.

———∞∞∞———

I walked hand-in-hand with my best Friend as He kept looking over at me with an almost-mischievous twinkle in His eyes. It was as if he was saying, *You're not gonna believe what I have to show you!* I was so completely and utterly fulfilled. Even though somehow I knew my family was grieving my absence, I was completely assured that Jesus was going to comfort them. Everything was just perfect.

My friends and family chattered excitedly as we all walked toward the mountains. As I talked to each of them, I noticed what seemed like a distinct glow over the next hill. As we reached the top of the hill I came to a sudden stop, trying to take in the view before me.

About a mile ahead of me, spread out across a huge plain, was the most astounding sight I had ever laid eyes on. I stood speechless and I blinked at a stunningly gorgeous, massive city that somehow glowed. I looked over at Jesus, who nodded with raised eyebrows as if to say, *Yes! The New Jerusalem!* I still had no words as I stood gaping at the immense beauty before me. The New Jerusalem had towers, arched columns, minarets, stepped walls, hanging gardens, and what even looked like suburbs with sprawling estates. People were bustling about as far as the eye could see, and I realized what was glowing. The streets were made of solid gold. I had read about the golden streets in the Bible, but seeing a city *glow* from the shine is something else altogether! Children seemed to be playing and dancing on the outskirts to what faintly sounded like the most beautiful melody of bells, stringed instruments, and voices. It was almost overwhelming.

"Danielle, do you want to see your estate?" Jesus asked. Of course, He had to know the answer before even asking.

"My ESTATE?" I squealed.

He laughed and said, "I know you know the scripture, 'In My Father's house are many mansions...'"

"Well, yeah...but..." I stammered as a hundred realizations flew through my mind. All the scriptures of promises Jesus gave us were literally true. I believed the promises. It was just weird seeing it in reality.

"Well, go on!" Jesus laughed. He had to know what I wanted to do more than anything else.

I laughed back and dashed madly down the hill toward the glowing city, skipping and dancing and twirling through a million flowers as I ran. I squealed again as I saw Jesus chasing right behind me. As I looked into His dazzling eyes, I knew that everything was just going to keep getting better and better and one day, in the timing of my Lord's perfect will, I would be dancing just like this with my precious family.

One of Danielle's best friends, Natalie, stepped up to the pulpit. She greeted everyone, and although her face was red from crying, she spoke as though she was completely in control. "I want to share with you today," she began, "not only what meant most to Danielle in this world..." she paused for a moment, "...but also Who made her the loving, caring and unforgettable person she was...*and still is.*"

Those last three words hung in the air almost tangibly.

"You see, Danielle had a personal relationship with her Lord and Savior, Jesus Christ."

Natalie continued to share some precious memories of Danielle and then she used the remainder of her time to share the Gospel. This hope of being reunited in Heaven through a decision to trust in Christ was an extremely powerful message for the hundreds of students and young adults there. I knew the message was sinking in deeply to previously unreached hearts. It was exactly what Danielle would have wanted.

Next, a video of Danielle's life played, while "Come to Jesus" by Chris Rice served as a soundtrack. As the lyrics sang of flying home in peace and laughing with Jesus on the other side of eternity, I closed my eyes, just wishing I could glimpse her laughing one more time. As I sat there, just taking in the song, I remembered the gift I had received the evening of the accident: the picture of my precious Danielle in the arms of Jesus. The song and video eventually faded out and I dabbed my eyes again and looked up to see Jon Overlie, a youth leader at our church, stand up to share the following words:

It was my privilege to be Danielle's Youth Leader through all four years of high school, here at Plymouth Covenant Church. As with all of you, I am grieving the loss of a wonderful child of God whom I loved.

Nowhere in the Bible are we told not to grieve. The Bible is filled with many stories of grieving people. However, the Bible encourages us not to grieve like people who have no hope. For since we believe that Jesus died and was raised to life again, we also believe that when Jesus returns, God will bring back with Him the believers who have died. As a follower of Jesus Christ, hope makes all the difference at a time like this. I know that Danielle has crossed from death to life. I know as a fact that she chose to accept God's free gift of salvation through faith in Jesus Christ. I know as fact that Danielle loved God and strived to know Him more. She's with God in eternity.

I've been blessed to work with a lot of wonderful students through youth group. Sometimes a student comes along who captures a piece of your heart. You get them, and they get you. For me, Danielle was one of those kids. Within our annual program, one of the most important things that we do is our annual mission trip. In three of the four years that Danielle was active in our ministry, she was on my small group team. On the one year that I did not go, she was in my wife, Michelle's group. It was amazing to see God show her who she was in Him on every trip and to see her take big steps toward God each time.

When I remember Danielle, the first thing that always comes to my mind is her smile. I simply cannot picture her in my mind with any facial expression other than a big grin. Danielle smiled when she was joyful, when she was anxious, when she was sure of something, when she wasn't. She probably even smiled when she was angry. I believe that smile of hers drew others to her—and it happened wherever she went. As a youth ministry, one of our principles is to include everyone. Danielle could do that like no other. She saw the best in everyone, saw their potential, no matter what they looked like on the outside. She loved inviting other students to youth group and was a wonderful example of reaching out to others.

Jesus calls us to minister to the "least"—the poor, hungry, thirsty, sick, and imprisoned. I can honestly say that Danielle was at her best when she was serving "the least," carrying out the mission of Jesus. In every mission experience, Danielle could always be found holding the dirtiest, grubbiest kid, playing tag with older kids until she could no longer stand, boldly entering people's homes to pray with them, holding babies, and not wanting to leave. She was at her best when she was serving in the mission field and at home serving the "least." She was who God created her to be. We talked of it often.

I really want to encourage everyone that the best way to honor Danielle is to reach out to others no matter where you are. Hug a dirty kid. Smile warmly at everyone you see. See others how God sees them, not how they look on the outside. I can imagine her smiling from Heaven at you.

Danielle, I love you and I'll miss you. I am so glad that one day, when I die, I will see your joyful, shining face again.

After the service was complete and the guests had all eaten lunch, a limousine took us to the cemetery. Another moment of shock hit me like a brick wall again. Was I really driving in a funeral procession following a hearse that carried the body of my precious daughter? As we approached the cemetery, I could feel myself becoming more anxious, and began to feel nauseous. The beautifully landscaped cemetery proved to be little comfort, but with groves of trees and a pond off to the side, surrounded by colorful, flowering hedges, at least it was a fitting site for my beautiful daughter's body. I staggered out of the limo and walked over to the gravesite.

Once all our friends and family had arrived and gathered around the grave, my brother Paul shared some final, parting words. The time had come for the mourners to say their final goodbyes. I watched as one of the most heart-wrenching moments I have ever experienced unfolded before me. Nathan picked up a perfect, pink rose, walked over to the grave and started peeling off the rose petals one by one, dropping them into the grave. His entire body was shaking as he sobbed loudly throughout this resolute display of absolute love and devotion for his sister. He drew the attention of all the other mourners, and those who had managed to fight back the tears now found it impossible. When he had dropped the last petal into the grave, Ashley walked over to him and they embraced, both now sobbing. I stood entirely devastated as I watched a brother and sister whose lives would never be the same without their cherished big sister.

Chapter Four:

A DELICATE TENSION

———— ∞∞ ————

T he weeks following the funeral were little more than a
haze of grief, with my mind swinging between sadness
and disbelief. Sandwiched somewhere between these alternating mindsets was the realization that life must continue
in spite of our grief. It was in this time that I read *A Grace
Disguised* by Jerry Sittser. Jerry had been the victim of a
horrific car accident involving a drunk driver. The other car
crossed into his lane, causing a head-on collision. His wife,
daughter, and mother all died in the accident. A statement
Jerry makes in this book aptly described my feelings at the
time: "Loss requires that we live in a delicate tension. We
must mourn, but we must go on living."[2]

A few days after the funeral, I attended one of Ashley's
soccer games. It was a beautiful evening, the floodlit field a
jumble of colors as the girls competed for the ball. A week
earlier, I would have reveled in the good weather while thoroughly enjoying the game. I would have chatted with the
other moms and cheered enthusiastically for the girls. Now
my life, attitude, and perspective had drastically changed.

I looked around at all the other spectators, thinking, *How
can everyone just act as if everything is normal when my
life is at a breaking point? Do they not see that my life has
just been shattered?* It wasn't a fair thought by any means,

but nothing was rational at that point. Somehow, I knew it was coming from a longing to have my other daughter back, a type of envy of the other moms, I suppose. I moved my chair as far down the sidelines as possible so I could still watch Ashley play while I broke down into involuntary bouts of tears. I didn't feel like talking to anyone, so I deliberately isolated myself from the parents. It felt like I was carrying a sign that said: *The mom who lost her daughter.*

As I sat watching Ashley dribble the ball skillfully around the other team's players, my heart broke for her, too. Earlier, while holding back her tears, she had asked me, "Do you think Danielle will be watching me play?" I told her I believed that Danielle was rooting for her from her balcony seat.

Just before I left for the game, I grabbed a notebook from Danielle's room because I found comfort in anything Danielle had written. During half-time I opened the notebook, and as I flipped through the pages I came across this Bible verse that Danielle had penned into her notebook: "Even though I walk through the valley of the shadow of death, I will fear no evil, for you are with me; your rod and your staff, they comfort me." (Psalm 23:4)

As my tears fell onto the pages of the notebook, I silently prayed, *God, I know You are with me, I just don't feel Your presence right now.* I yearned for God's comforting touch, but I felt nothing. By this point I was shaking in an attempt to suppress my pent-up sobbing. Even though I had deliberately chosen to sit far away from the others, one of the other soccer moms walked over, hugged me, and said she had just been praying that I would feel God's comfort. I could only nod and say a raspy, "Thanks," but as she walked away, I thanked God for continuing to show me that He cares.

Back at home that evening, I remembered the question Ashley had asked earlier about whether Danielle was watching her play soccer. I picked up Randy Alcorn's book, *Heaven* and looked up the section entitled: *Do people in the present Heaven see what is happening on earth?* This is what I read:

> If the martyrs in Heaven know that God hasn't yet brought judgment on their persecutors (Revelation 6:9-11), it seems evident that the inhabitants of the present Heaven can see what's happening on Earth, at least to some extent..."There is rejoicing in the presence of the angels of God over one sinner who repents" (Luke 15:10). Notice it does not speak of rejoicing by the angels but in the presence of angels. Who is doing this rejoicing in Heaven? I believe it logically includes not only God but also the saints in Heaven, who would so deeply appreciate the wonder of human conversion—especially the conversion of those they knew and loved on earth. If they rejoice over conversions happening on Earth, then obviously *they must be aware of what is happening on Earth*—and not just generally, but specifically, down to the details of individuals coming to faith in Christ.[3]

Can I infer from this Bible passage that Danielle was definitely watching the soccer game? Not necessarily. However, it does bring me comfort to think that God may allow her to see some events that occur here on Earth.

The next day I went into Danielle's room, still piled with boxes of her stuff from her Bethel dorm room. Just entering her room reduced me to tears. One of Danielle's favorite sweatshirts was lying on top of one of the boxes. Fresh tears flooded my eyes as I picked it up and hugged it. Oh, how I wished I were hugging Danielle. I thought back to Mother's Day less than two weeks earlier, and clung to the memory of hugging my daughter as she was leaving for Bethel. Never could I have imagined that the hug would be the last I would ever have from her on this earth. We take so many things for granted.

I moved a few things off her desk and through my tears, I noticed a stack of sealed envelopes. I picked a couple up and felt a little card inside each one. On the envelopes were written the names of people to whom these cards were addressed. I thought perhaps Danielle was planning a party and these were the invitations that had not yet been sent. I opened the first one:

> Thanks for being such a good friend. You always have a smile on your face and bring joy to so many, including me. Always remember how much God loves you and wants to know you so much more on a personal level. Stay close to God daily. I'm praying for you. Danielle ♥

That opened a floodgate of tears that poured down my face. I continued to open the cards one by one. Each started out with a specific encouragement and ended with words similar to the first card. After reading the last card I sat there sobbing again, painfully missing my gem, my Danielle. Yet I also felt like God had just sent me another gift by allowing me to read those cards. I was so thankful that Danielle hadn't already given the letters to her friends. A few weeks later, I found out that the cards were addressed to friends from Bethel. Danielle was most likely going to hand the cards to them or put them in their mailboxes. I sent the cards to the respective people they were addressed to and included a copy of a letter I composed:

> Hi, Danielle must have really appreciated you— for you were one of the friends that she wrote to before she went home to her Heavenly Father. My prayer is that God will use you in an incredible way. I miss our beautiful Danielle so very much,

but I know she's in a much better place and someday we'll be reunited.

I heard back from some of her friends who talked about Danielle's life and how she had influenced them in a positive way. At the time, I had no idea that God was going to eventually use these notes to start a ministry.

As the weeks trundled along, a very significant concern I had was how this tragedy would affect Ashley and Nathan. They were both so young at the time, and to have to deal with such sadness in life, especially at such a tender age, carries the potential of emotional scarring. Pre-teens and teens can bring a complicated emotional package to their sadness, and need careful attention, reassurance, and support.

A few weeks after the accident I was sitting with Ashley in her bedroom, just having a mother and daughter talk, and she suddenly began crying, visibly wracked with exceptional despair.

Through her sobs she cried out, "Who will be my maid of honor at my wedding? Who will I tell when I'm excited about something?"

My heart ached for her as she lamented the many dreams she had shared with her sister that would now never be fulfilled. As she wept in my arms, all I could do was pray for God to comfort her. As a mom, I wanted desperately to fix this for my children—to make the pain go away. But I couldn't.

After about ten minutes she suddenly quieted down and then looked up. I saw such blessed peace shining from her eyes that had not been there moments before.

She said, "Mom, Dani will never be sad again, will she?"

I replied through my tears, "No, honey, she will never again experience any sadness or hurt for the rest of eternity."

Although Ashley had known this truth in her mind, God had now cemented it in her heart. I quietly thanked Him for giving Ashley the comfort she needed at that time.

Nathan's class at Heritage Christian Academy had put together a book in which all the students had written cards to Nathan, many with Bible verses. It was a beautiful gesture and revealed how much they all cared. Shortly after he had received this special gift from his classmates, I walked into his room and found him re-reading the cards. My eyes filled with tears as I pleaded, *Oh God, please comfort Nathan. He has lost his big sister—his snowboarding buddy.* I asked him what he was reading and he showed me a card with Revelation 21:4 written on it: "He will wipe every tear from their eyes. There will be no more death or mourning or crying or pain." I could tell he was clinging to this with all of his heart. To this day, Nathan regards this as his favorite verse.

During those first months, I was living within a strange, delicate tension of grieving while continuing to live life. Along with that came an uncertainty about my emotions. Deep pain surfaced at unique times. I found myself feeling fine and even believing I was making progress in overcoming the grief when, suddenly, I would see or hear something that ambushed me with sorrow. I found myself spiraling into a vortex of anger, sorrow, and a miriad of other raw emotions.

One such triggering experience was shopping at Target, where Danielle had worked. It took many months before I could shop there without experiencing significant emotion. While at Target a few months after the accident, I was looking for an item and my eyes were so clouded with tears that I couldn't see it. As tears were streaming down my cheeks, one of the employees came up, and seeing me crying, she sweetly asked if she could help me find something. After she found the item, she gently touched my arm and said that she would pray for me.

Although she had no idea why I was crying, her kindness gave me encouragement. At the time I was too distraught to think of this, but as I later documented this touching story in my journal, I wondered what was happening in the invisible world at that time. I think we are going to be amazed when we get to Heaven and find out how often our Heavenly Father intervened with circumstances we chalked up to random acts of kindness. It's truly wonderful when we see God's love in action. It shows that He cares for us on every level, and it was also a reminder to me that we should always be willing to listen to the Holy Spirit when He nudges us to do something.

Shopping at Target also reminds me of a hilarious experience with Danielle. She had a strong sense of humor, and an incident that took place at Target makes me laugh, even today. Before the accident, I had received one of those emails that people forward on, titled "50 crazy things you can do at Wal-Mart." Well, Danielle decided she just had to try one of these ideas. One day Danielle and I were in Target on a day she wasn't working, and she spotted a new employee whom she hadn't met yet.

With an impish twinkle in her eye she waddled up to the young man, and crossing her legs, asked him loudly and desperately, "Will you *PLEASE* tell me where I can find tampons?" He was absolutely mortified and just stood there, speechless. Then Danielle broke character and slapped him on the shoulder, cracking up. She told him she was just kidding and she worked there too. I couldn't help but laugh and the young man seemed to immediately take it well. That was Danielle. She brought joy to every situation.

One evening while downstairs, I glanced over at my children's books stacked on a shelf. There was one that immediately caught my eye and, flushed with excitement, I picked it up. It was one of Danielle's favorites, called *Shadows and Shining Lights.*[4] It was an imaginative book about two children who meet their guardian angel, who helps them understand that he is sent by God to protect them. I must have read this book to Danielle twenty-five to thirty times. We had fun imagining what her angel looked like and how busy her angel was watching over her. I turned the first page in the book and Psalm 91:11 was printed in large bold letters, "For he will command his angels concerning you to guard you in all your ways." I read through the book tear-fully, and at the end I thought, *Well Danielle, your guardian angel no longer has to protect you. You are safe.*

———∞———

I couldn't help breaking into a full sprint for the last hundred yards to reach the golden city. As I ran I watched several children playing in trees, chasing each other around them. They sensed my curiosity and stopped to wave as I dashed by.

Finally I came to a road that just seemed to begin from under the grass. I knelt, not even breathing heavily from my sprint, and touched the first brick. Pure gold. I whirled around to my group, who were still lagging behind. Jesus smiled and nodded. I touched a few more bricks and knocked on one of them. It was solid.

Wow! I thought.

"You just arrived, didn't you?" a child asked.

I looked up surprised, but smiled at the face of a beautiful little girl with the biggest, brown eyes. She looked Middle Eastern.

"Yes, I did," I said. "How long have you been here?"

"Feels like I just got here, but also feels like I've been here forever." She giggled.

I chuckled in response, understanding what she meant. I really couldn't tell in terms of minutes on an earthly clock how long I'd been here. I'd experienced so much already, and yet it all still felt so beautifully new.

"Rida, my special girl!" Jesus walked up next to us. "Did you know Danielle here supported friends of your family?"

"Oh, Jesus!" she cried as she saw Him, and threw her arms around His leg. He laughed and knelt, and then squeezed her tightly.

"Rida lived in the Persian Gulf. Her parents are missionaries there, and you sent a support gift to some associates of her folks." Jesus stood up.

"I remember giving in that offering. The missionaries spoke at our church once," I said thoughtfully. "What a small world." I was about to ask how Rida had arrived in Heaven when she jumped up and down, holding her arms up to Jesus.

"Lord Jesus, come and play. Come and PLAY!"

He scooped her up like a feather, laughing again, and kissed her on the cheek. "I have to show Danielle something special, but I'll come back in a little while and we can play tag, okay?"

"Okay," she said, smiling up at Him and swinging out the bottom of her little white dress.

By now the other children had realized Jesus was there too and had formed a happy, noisy, little mob around us. They were all jumping up and down, and begging Jesus to come and play with them. It was the most beautiful sight. Rida took the lead and said, "Jesus promised to come back in a little while and play tag with us!"

"Oh, okay," they all said in unison, and then started yelling how much they loved Jesus and couldn't wait till He came back.

I knew exactly how they felt. I could hang out with Him forever and it wouldn't be enough. Every second I spent with Him, I fell in love with Him more.

"Danielle, I'm going to go ahead and get something ready for you, okay?" Jesus said to me, reassuringly. "I love you, Rida, I'll be back later!" Jesus promised, and knelt down and gave her another squeeze. She batted her big, brown eyes at Him and smiled in total bliss. Then He smiled at me and headed toward a rather large tower on the edge of the city.

Until now, I either hadn't seen or hadn't been aware of the presence of the big man who had lifted me out of the car and brought me here. I turned and he was standing a little way off, watching Jesus go toward the tower. I smiled at him and waved and he smiled back and walked over.

"Our Lord is truly magnificent, isn't He?" he said.

"Oh, I love Him so much!" I said. "There is just no one like Him."

"There is no one like Him!" the man echoed and added, "Praise be to the living God Jehovah!"

"Praise be to the living God Jehovah!" my friends and family shouted. I felt another rush of joy as we praised our God.

"Who *are* you?" I asked.

He smiled and asked, "You really don't know?"

"You're my...guardian angel?"

He nodded. "Yes, Danielle. I've been assigned to you since your birth."

I realized why he looked so familiar...actually he didn't *look* familiar, instead his presence was familiar.

"Wow." I nodded. "I feel like I know you, but we haven't really met."

"Oh, we've met." He smiled. "But I was always more of a silent partner, I suppose you could say. I was always there, though."

"What's your name?"

"Well, you and your mom decided to call me *Joy* one day..."

"Joy! That's right!" I exclaimed. I remembered sitting on the bed with my mom, reading *Shadows and Shining Lights,* discussing what my guardian angel was like. "I thought you were a *girl!*" I exclaimed.

"I *know!*" he said, with a grin. "Surprise!" He held his hands out as if to display with no mistake that he was masculine. I laughed loudly. "In fact, you weren't far off you know." He smiled.

"Really?" I asked. "What's your name?"

"Simcha," he said, with a giant smile. He seemed proud of his name.

"Simcha?" I asked, trying to pronounce it correctly. He nodded. "What does it mean?"

"Ah. That can be your homework. I'll give you a clue, though. You can ask one of the Hebrew people."

"Aww!" I groaned, but I could see he wouldn't tell me. "Wow," I said thoughtfully. "So you were there the entire time?"

"Yes," he replied, reverting back to his official tone.

"So, you know me pretty well then, right?"

"Toward a certain extent, yes, I know your tendencies. I couldn't pretend to know the depths of the human spirit, however."

"So you should know, then, what I am thinking right now as I gaze at the mountains?"

He looked up at the distant, snowy mountain peaks, stretching up toward the sky.

"Danielle, those peaks have the softest powder you've ever seen, and the most mind-blowing runs and lines. My dear, you are in for some spectacular snowboarding!"

"OH!" I shouted. "That's amazing! How do you know what I'm thinking?"

He chuckled a bit and then maintained his official, angelic composure again. "You don't even need a helmet!" he added, leaning in like it was a bit of confidential information.

"So do you know how to snowboard?"

"Do I know how to snowboard?" He laughed. "Who do you think turned you *just enough* on the more-than-a-few occasions you were heading for some trees or rocks?"

"Hmm! Yeah, I remember some really close calls." I laughed, thinking back at how I thought I was just *lucky*. "You must have really had your hands full with me, huh?"

"Let's just say, in our Lord's supreme wisdom, I believe I was assigned to you because I enjoy adventure." He smiled again.

I really liked my angel. He was cool, and I realized now how many times he must have saved me. I knew intuitively, however, that he was not to be worshiped. He was a servant of our great God, and although I could tell he was good, and very powerful, he was not to be deified. He seemed to sense my thoughts and nodded. I could tell he knew his purpose, and was happy to be in the obedient service of his King.

I looked down for a few seconds and then asked, "So what happened on the night I left earth?"

He breathed in deeply, exhaled, and then said, "Danielle, I can only serve within the parameters I am given, and believe me, it was painful for me to watch you experience even the slightest bit of fear. Nevertheless, I could do only what I was able to."

This was a fairly cryptic answer, but I somehow knew the gist of what he meant. I was completely comfortable with the fact that all the answers would be revealed to me in time.

Suddenly I sensed an urgency throughout my entire being. I saw my angel sensed it too and acknowledged it with his eyes.

He then said, "Let me show you something," and touched my hand. Instantly it was as though a giant projector screen appeared in front of us. As though I were watching a movie, I saw my mom and Ashley sitting on her bed. Ashley was sobbing.

"Who will be my maid of honor at my wedding? Who will I tell when I'm excited about something?" she cried.

My mom put her arm around her and clearly didn't know what to say. Then I saw something very strange. Out of my mom's heart, wispy, golden words floated up toward Heaven, and I could read what they said.

"Oh God, please comfort Ashley. She is so young. Please protect her. You're the only one who can help her. Please Lord, just comfort her."

The words trailed up, looking like incense drifting, and curling their way to Heaven. I was in awe, but then snapped out of it.

"We have to do something!" I cried. "ASHLEY! I'M OKAY!" I shouted. Neither of them acknowledged my voice. I desperately wanted to reassure Ashley—to tell her that what really matters is her relationship with Jesus. I wanted her to know the Savior is so wonderful and I'm having the time of my life! "How do I help her?" I yelled to Simcha.

"Be at peace, Danielle," he said softly. "They are in very capable hands. The Master Himself makes intercession for them. Even now, Jehovah has heard your mother's prayers. The mighty Holy Spirit will comfort your family."

I looked at him, knowing what he said was true, but I could still see Ashley suffering.

"Look." He motioned with his hand toward the shimmering vision before us. A breeze seemed to rustle through the room and I saw the most beautiful, almost translucent white dove gently flapping its wings. It hovered in front of Ashley for a few seconds and then softly perched on her lap. Slowly, an iridescent, gorgeously colorful mist swirled from the dove and seemed to cloak Ashley as she sniffed and wiped her eyes.

She looked up at my mom and said, "Mom, Dani will never be sad again, will she?"

"No, never Ash!" I knew she couldn't hear me, but I shouted anyway. "I've never been so happy!"

"No honey, she will never again experience any sadness or hurt for the rest of eternity," my mom answered her, and took Ashley's hands in her own.

The rainbow-colored, smoky mist was now swirling around my mom too, and the dove slowly flapped Its wings and hovered in front of both of them. I was mesmerized. I saw another prayer floating up from my mom's heart. It was a prayer of thanks, and I could tell this really blessed the dove. I finally exhaled with a sigh of relief, so happy that my family knew and trusted our great God. I wished I could tell them how amazing Heaven was, but I rested in the fact that our precious Jesus and His wonderful Holy Spirit were in charge of comforting them.

Chapter Five:

THE STRUGGLE

———⌘———

T he night of the accident, when the officer first communicated the news, I heard none of the details due to being in shock. I remember the excruciating pain I felt when I was told that Danielle had been drinking alcohol. To an already grief-stricken mom, this additional blow sent me reeling. It was like a dagger in my heart, thinking Danielle losing her life could have been avoided.

I later found out Danielle had attended a party that night to celebrate the end of finals. A few girls came up to me at the funeral and they were shaking as they emotionally described their last conversation with Danielle at the party. They spoke of her excitement for summer, wanting to meet them to go rollerblading (a favorite activity of Danielle's). One mentioned with tears rolling down her face that Danielle encouraged her that night and said she'd be praying for her.

She added in a grief-stricken voice, "We shouldn't have been drinking."

I just held the poor girl, and the two of us wept together. One, a brokenhearted mom, and the other, a grieving friend experiencing tremendous regret.

After having some time to process everything and think a little, I began to feel a great burden of guilt sweeping over me as I thought about what I could have done differently to prevent the accident. Could I have done a better job in instilling values? If I had prayed more intensely or stayed closer to God, could I have prevented this? I remember being completely broken, questioning the choices I had made in parenting Danielle. I allowed my mind to think of all the families I knew, in whose lives it seemed everything was perfect. They didn't have a precious daughter who had made a poor choice that cost her life. Where did I go wrong?

Guilt became a terrible weight I carried, and it became clear I had to make a choice: wallow in guilt and allow it to steal my joy, or give it to God and ask Him to heal me. I finally broke down and asked God to set me free from the guilt I was feeling. I felt a sense of peace that I realized came from God.

In the following few days, God again used some of Danielle's writings to minister to me. Going through Danielle's desk one evening, I found a devotional book and journal that she had written in her senior year of high school. As I read it, it showed the internal struggle Danielle was feeling in her life. She wrote:

> Dear Jesus, I want to focus on you and have you take 100% control over my life. I want to spend more time with you praying and reading the Bible. But I struggle with sinful thoughts and actions. Please help me.

Danielle was always open with her feelings, including her desire to live fully committed to God, yet like many young people, struggled with being pulled into the world. Her last day on this earth demonstrated this struggle, having recently written cards to friends encouraging them to stay close to God, yet making choices that evening that ultimately took her life. As I reflect on that evening, I can't help but think about the spiritual battle that was going on for Danielle's life.

Simcha took his hand off my shoulder and the vision sort of evaporated. I felt at peace, knowing that my mom and Ashley, and my whole family for that matter, were being taken care of by God. One thing still troubled me, though. Simcha had obviously been there when my body was broken, and I couldn't help but wonder.

"Why didn't you stop the accident?" I asked him bluntly.

After a few seconds, he inhaled slowly and deeply. He turned to look me square in the eyes, but his gaze was full of compassion. I could also tell it was uncomfortable for him to talk about the accident. I wondered if he felt as though he failed.

"I didn't fail," he said, obviously guessing what I was thinking. "It's more like I was unable to protect you."

I looked at him in surprise. The thought hadn't even occurred to me. Surely he was able to protect me if God so empowered him?

"Danielle, many believers often allow things to take place that should never happen."

"You mean I *allowed* the wreck?" I exclaimed, but as the words came out of my mouth, I immediately knew what he meant. Why had I done something as stupid as drink and drive? "But why couldn't you have protected me anyway? I've had a lot of close calls before this. Jetskiing. Rollerblading. You name it. I'm sure there were many more times you saved me than what I'm aware of!"

"Jesus gives mankind grace, but there is always a risk with an overt disregard for the Word of God."

"What was I thinking that night? I knew what I was doing was wrong."

"There were adversaries," he replied. His jaw clenched and there was a brief flash of anger in his eyes.

"Adversaries?" I asked, puzzled. "Like enemies?" I was really confused. I remembered when he lifted me out of the car there were no other people in sight.

"Even before the accident," he said. I could tell he was highly disciplined in remaining calm, but there was a definite battle-ready look about him at the moment. Something about the time preceding the accident made him bristle.

"Please tell me what happened," I begged. He was looking at the ground now, and then looked into my eyes again.

"I would show you if I could, but you would be horrified at their twisted forms," he said abruptly. "They seduced you and their intent was to destroy you." His jaw was clenched again.

"Like..." I paused as the truth came over me. "Demons?" I asked, with my hand covering my mouth. He nodded and a look of disgust crossed his face.

"The mere power of suggestion," he said, looking at the ground again.

Now it made sense. These adversaries must have been planting thoughts in my mind. I remembered feeling that I wanted to have fun and party with my friends. I thought I was totally fine to get in the car and drive. But I had allowed monstrous beings—enemies of my Lord—to intervene in my life. How could I have been so duped?

I felt absolutely no guilt, nor any condemnation, because I instinctively knew I was forgiven and free. I did, however, wonder about the lives I could have impacted.

Simcha anticipated my concern. "The Lord redeems the time, Danielle. He is already beginning to use your testimony and your witness to reach those you left behind."

"But how?" I asked.

"God has planted the seeds of a ministry in your mom's heart," he answered with an undertone of victory.

I almost did a back flip. Instead of a sense of loss, pure joy flooded my heart. In God's unfathomable love and grace, He was still using what I left behind to reach others. I just wanted to sing about how His ways were truly astounding. Simcha was smiling now too, as he saw I grasped it. Beating me to it, he broke out into a song of praise to the Lord, and in perfect unison, I joined him. Soon I heard voices all around us joining in.

Randy Alcorn describes the type of dialogue that Satan and his evil forces engage in with Christians. He points out how it started during that first encounter with Eve:

> Satan often appears as an angel of light (2 Corinthians 11:14)—appearing beautiful, enticing... He whispers to us as he did to Eve: 'Question God. Reinterpret God's command. Don't take seriously his warnings following sin. Don't worry; evil won't have consequences. God is withholding good from you. You don't need God. You can call your own shots.[5]

It is tempting to be angry with Danielle for falling into the lies that suggested there would be no consequences for her choice. I gain comfort from humbly recognizing my own inclinations toward poor choices (Romans 3:23) and being grateful that God's mercy and grace ensure that even poor choices are redeemed for good purposes when we love God (Romans 8:28).

On this side of Heaven, God gives us opportunities to see some blessings—ways that God is redeeming the horror of the spiritual battle that seemed lost on May 17th. Despite how it may look and feel on the surface of the circumstances, God is still bringing good out of Danielle's death. One of the ways He is doing that is by putting Danielle's story in front of young people and empowering them to be overcomers.

Often Danielle's mangled car is placed right outside of a school. This has a tremendous impact on students. Seeing that crumpled car, the twisted metal, and the shattered glass causes them to stop for a moment and face the possibilities. Pretty quickly, it knocks the wind out their sense of invincability and reduces the allure of seemingly harmless drinking. Reality hits closer to home when you can see and touch that crushed driver's side door.

I regularly hear conversations afterward and see on students' faces that lives are being changed. It strengthens my faith to know that other lives may be spared in the aftermath of Danielle's mistakes. So even as God is redeeming this story on campuses around the country, he is redeeming my mourning with vision for His eternal purposes. What a gift. What joy!

Chapter Six:

THE ALL-ENCOMPASSING PLAN
OF GOD

⸺⸰⸰⸺

I faced a very emotional decision a few weeks after the accident. We were contemplating donating Danielle's car to MADD (Mothers Against Drunk Driving). It was a decision over which I wrestled with God. Danielle's story, which would be posted on the car, would communicate that she made the choice to drink and drive, which ultimately cost her life. I was humbled in a way I had not been before, and part of me wanted to simply hide in my denial. As I prayed about it, God began to deeply deal with my pride.

As I was praying, Genesis 50:20 came to me. Joseph, the second most powerful man in Egypt, replied to his brothers: "You intended to harm me, but God intended it for good to accomplish what is now being done, the saving of many lives." The verse reminded me that yes, Satan intended the tragedy for harm, but God will use it to accomplish the saving of many lives (physically, but much more important, eternally).

It wasn't the first time I'd struggled with the question, "How could anything good come out of this?" A few days after Danielle's funeral, I reflected in my journal on the unbelievable sadness I was experiencing and how I just couldn't make any sense out of her death. I wrote Romans 8:28 and asked God how He was going to fashion good out of this. "And we know that in all things God works for the good of those who love him, who have been called according to his purpose."

A critical question I had to answer was whether I really believed God's promise in this scripture. Eventually I was able to reconcile the verse with my doubt and completely believe the Lord's promise. Romans 8:28 doesn't tell me I should say, "It is good that Danielle died in the car accident," but rather when the Bible says, "for good," God implies ultimate and eternal good, not necessarily how we often interpret "good" in reference to our personal happiness. Yes, God often blesses us in this world and turns our adversities to our advantage. But ultimately He desires our spiritual development and eternal "good." Having a comfortable life is not God's chief aim for me. He sees the big picture and wants to form me more and more into the image of His Son.

The day after I journaled my struggles with Romans 8:28, I found the cards that Danielle had written to her friends. I wrote in my journal that I felt God was saying, *Melody, this is part of the answer to your Romans 8:28 question. Go and use these cards to reach others!* These cards became the motivation to create a website that is reaching thousands of people.

As difficult as it was for me to surrender to God, and donate Danielle's car to MADD, I eventually relented and obeyed Him. Her car is driven on a trailer to many different locations throughout the spring, summer, and fall, and is impacting many people. One of the first letters I received after donating the car was this one:

> Hi Melody, I am writing to thank you for sharing Danielle's story and car with us through the MADD Crash Car Program. I coordinated an alcohol awareness day for our company and wanted to let you know that Danielle's story touched over 230 lives yesterday alone. Many of our associates have also mentioned that they have visited Danielle's website and have been touched by the pieces of

her life that you let people experience through her web page.

I can't tell you how much feedback from others encouraged me. I was blessed to receive these gifts that clearly showed how God could turn tragedy into a life-saver for others.

When we worked with MADD to write the sign for Danielle's car, an essential aspect of the message we wanted conveyed was to challenge people on their choices and highlight the consequences of drinking and driving. I was also interested in using Danielle's story to reach those who may not know the saving power of our Lord Jesus. This "eternal" message was communicated through Danielle's website, which is also posted on the car. I praise the Lord for how He has used the website. At the time I wrote this, the website had over 11,000 hits. I assume that the majority have been due to students and others seeing Danielle's car. If I take Danielle's accident by itself, it is sense-less. But I realize that after God has worked out His perfect design, even this calamity will be used in a redemptive way.

I had an opportunity to hear Carol Kent speak and was touched by her story. Carol's life changed drastically with the news that her son, Jason, had killed his wife's ex-husband for fear that he would hurt her two daughters, whom he loved deeply. The murder came as a complete shock to everyone who knew Jason. He was sentenced to life in prison, without the possibility of parole. Out of this a ministry has been formed that reaches out to inmates and their families. This statement by Carol in her book, *A New Kind Of Normal*, resonated with me deeply as I reflected on how God was making good out of the evil Satan desired:

> When we fully understand that we are in a spiritual battle, that the world is not our home, just a "stopping off" place, we can begin to get excited about having a short time to engage in the battle raging around us. The enemy wants us to waste our time generating anger toward others, ruminating

over personal betrayals and over injustices due to sickness, accidents, and evil. He wants to destroy our ability to function productively and to disengage us from inspiring others to be Christ-followers.[6]

Carol also spoke about how she made herself available by being vulnerable, through sharing with others the imperfect situations in her life. She states, "*Fear taunts*, people will reject you and make you feel like a flawed person. *Faith says,* take the risk, be real, allow God to use the broken places of your past to give hope to someone else."[7]

I could relate. I found that being open and vulnerable creates a magnet within me that draws those who are hurting. God has shown me that my brokenness and pain can be used for others' healing.

Joseph, who I mentioned earlier, is an excellent example of a man of faith, and his story shows how good can come out of suffering. Joseph was hated by his brothers, sold as a slave, accused of attempted rape, and put into prison for years. He remained faithful to God even though there were probably many times when he wondered where God was in his suffering. Joseph didn't see how God was working behind the scenes, but God had a purpose that Joseph was unaware of. In the end, Joseph realized God's intentions had always been good. Ultimately God raised up Joseph to become the prime minister of Egypt and save many lives.

Notice that God did not provide an explanation to Joseph concerning why he was going through all of those years of suffering. Similarly, many of us also live out our days on earth without answers to the "Whys?" In many cases, until we get to Heaven, we will not fully understand the complex intertwining of events in the role God has for us in His story. Don't get discouraged if you can't see how God is going to bring good out of a tragedy, but simply trust Him, because God's ways are far beyond anything we can imagine. Someday you will understand how God redeemed your loss and caused it to work for eternal good.

As you look back over your life, ask yourself: When have you grown the most? Was it when everything was going well, or would you say, as I would, that the times of greatest growth and the greatest intimacy with Jesus have been in the midst of painful experiences? God used the accident to refine my faith as it has established a much deeper dependence on Him. I've learned to trust God even when His ways didn't make sense to me and I couldn't see what was ahead. Suffering has a way of grabbing our attention to learn things from God that we would never otherwise have learned. I have shared with a number of people that I wish I could have learned and grown as much as I did while still having Danielle alive. Unfortunately, if I'm painfully honest, I don't see how that could have happened.

Loss can provide us with an opportunity to take inventory of our lives. It can be a wake-up call, revealing that our priorities and goals are not as we want them to be. I like how Randy Alcorn explains this in his book, *If God Is Good*:

> When our lives here end, what will we wish we had done less of? And what will we wish we had done more of in order to honor God and build our character? Why not spend the rest of our lives closing the gap between what we've done for Christ and what we'll wish we had done?[8]

For me, Danielle's death was a wake-up call to remind me that life is fleeting. It instilled within me much more of a desire to reach others for Christ. There may be ways that God wants to use you, and is using a painful time in your life to prepare you.

An astonishing woman of faith, Joni Eareckson Tada, who has been a quadriplegic since a diving accident at the age of seventeen, has a powerful ministry that has touched so many lives throughout the world. While many individuals experiencing Joni's trials would have been in despair, her strong faith in the midst of her suffering has encouraged many. In her book, *The God I Love,* Joni says this to God: "I know I wouldn't know You...I wouldn't love and trust You...were it not for this wheelchair."[9] She firmly believes that the wheelchair that originally felt like a curse has actually given her a front row seat to the love and faithfulness of God. Personally, I agree with Joni in that through my painful suffering, I have seen the awesomeness of God that I probably would have never seen had my journey been smooth.

Although God uses suffering, it is not always easy when He does. It's exciting when your child does something that warrants a story in the newspaper. What parent doesn't love reading about their child's sports achievement, academic accomplishment, or artistic success? There were a number of times in the years following Danielle's accident, however, that her story made the paper, and this was definitely not how I wanted to see Danielle's name written up for people to read. On one of these occasions, the headline read: *Osseo Senior High School students get sobering reminder.*

The article went on to describe the alcohol-related accident and included three pictures of Danielle and the smashed car. This type of article, although heartbreaking, is a visible reminder of how God continues to use the tragedy to help others make wise choices.

A dear friend, Lisa Jamieson, showed great sensitivity to our family's vulnerability when Danielle's story was going to be in the news. She sent an email to several of my girlfriends asking for prayer. Here is what she wrote:

> Danielle's car appeared in the *Star-Tribune* this weekend along with an educational article aimed at reminding parents to help position their teens for safe choices about drinking. It's another powerful opportunity God will use to build awareness on so many levels—most of all shining light on the Gospel and God's loving desire for us to thrive in this life and beyond. Nonetheless, it is profoundly difficult for the family to have the ongoing vision of this car prompting them to face the heartbreak of their own

tragedy over and over again. Please read this article and note the photos of Danielle and the car. What a tribute to the legacy of a precious young woman who would consider it a privilege to participate in God's work bringing "beauty out of ashes." Particularly this month, with Mother's Day around the corner, the pain is so raw and overwhelming at times for Melody. Let's stand with them tonight, this week, this month in claiming VICTORY over destruction, the TRUTH of God's saving power and grace, and the JOY of knowing what hope eternity hold.[10]

We have a role in cooperating with the fulfillment of God's purpose in our suffering. I could have stayed stuck on trying to figure out the "Why?" question, or I could have allowed the fear of what others think keep me from creating Danielle's website. He may not be asking you to create a website or form a mission. He may just want you to radiate peace and joy when your dreams are shattered, or to remain faithful when you walk through the storms of life.

Many people say that they want the kind of life that causes others to say they see God through you, but this often comes with sacrifice. The good news is that when people see you walking through hardship and see the grace of God reflected in your spirit and words, they will be impacted. You can be light to a dark world, which is part of God's redeeming purpose for your suffering.

Someday we will realize that God doesn't waste our pain. It is difficult to view our suffering as fleeting, but ultimately, when we are with Jesus in Heaven, we will become aware of the fact that our sorrows were momentary in contrast to eternal joy and eternal rewards. Randy Alcorn's words in *If God Is Good,* resonates with me on this thought:

> You may feel your choices have been reduced to whether you want Jell-0, or a window opened, or an extra blanket. On the contrary, your choice of

whether you will trust God and worship him today reverberates throughout the universe, honoring or dishonoring your God. It also has enormous implications for eternal rewards God promises us in the next life.[11]

Everything that happens, including our painful experiences, is being woven together by God like a piece of tapestry. From an earthly perspective we see the underside of the tapestry, and it seems knotted, tangled, and twisted. God, however, sees the topside and creates a beautiful picture. Going through Danielle's tragedy initially seemed so confusing and meaningless, but I continue to trust God every day that His perfect plan is unfolding. I pray you can, too.

———— ∞ ————

Our spontaneous song slowed until it drifted into a beautiful, golden silence. Every moment in Heaven was filled with pure bliss and fresh wonder. It made me want to know more.

I whirled around and looked at Simcha, who smiled as he saw my eyes, which must have looked like a hungry kitten's, waiting for its treat.

"Ah, Danielle, you've always been so thirsty to understand!" He chuckled.

"So?" I cut straight to the point. "I have so many questions, Simcha—about life here and life on earth. How does this all make sense? Why do bad things happen to good people on earth? I know the Lord has reasons for allowing it, but I wish I could understand why."

"You know what a tapestry is, don't you?" he asked gently.

"Uhhh, yeah?" I answered, wondering where this was going.

"The front of a skillful tapestry is very intricate, detailed and beautiful, yes?" he continued.

"The front?" I asked. He just looked at me and so I frowned in a nice way but just nodded.

"Have you ever looked at the back of a tapestry, Danielle?" he asked.

Of course he knew I had. One of my friend's grandmothers had been quite good at needlework and had several of her embroidered pieces hanging on their walls. I had seen one of them in progress as she deftly handled her two round bands of bamboo that stretched the cloth tightly, so she could thread her patterns through. Then it clicked. One day she showed me the back of the cloth and I believe even said something to the effect of, "Isn't it amazing how tattered the back can look, while the front is so beautiful?" while looking over her bifocals, resting on her nose. I had smiled politely, but glossed over her words as pretty trite. I had no idea of the depth of her wisdom.

Simcha looked at me, visibly perceiving my thoughts. He had been there. He knew what I was recalling. He also knew that I was putting the pieces of the puzzle together.

"Life on earth sure isn't perfect, is it?" I said, looking away at the mountains.

"In any place where sin reigns, it can never be perfect," he said with a note of compassion in his voice.

"So is the front of the tapestry only here? In Heaven?" I asked.

He smiled, which surprised me. It seemed like a pretty solemn thought to me. "Think about it, dear girl. Many servants of our great God have run their race and finished their call. Every one of them suffered, and it may have seemed at times that they could only see the messy back side of the tapestry. However, the fruit of their work—their legacy—was very evident to see in their lifetime."

"So you're telling me, the front of the tapestry can be seen in life on earth too, and we can see the beauty of God's plan?" I half-yelled in excitement. "YAAAAAY!" I jumped up and down and hugged the angel impulsively.

He embraced me like I imagine my brother Nathan would, if he were seven feet tall. He was laughing now with me, and we were both excited at my new revelation.

I stood there for a second and took this all in. I could see now that it must have seemed tragic that I was a Christian, yet I made a poor choice. And then I died. But that was the messy back side of the tapestry. The tapestry's beauty didn't make sense that way. The front showed the witness the Lord could use for my generation against the dangers of alcohol, as well as a reminder that life is brief and to make sure we are ready for eternity.

"You left a legacy too, Danielle," Simcha said softly. I looked up at him. "So many lives touched through relationship with friends, through Bible studies, through prayer. You were doing your Lord's work even then."

"I guess I just had such big dreams. I was going to go on mission trips, maybe counsel people. You know—impact the world!" I paused for a second. I wasn't sad, but somehow my thoughts drifted back to my loved ones. "And what about my family? How will they understand?"

"Danielle, the Holy Spirit is already ministering to them. They are strong enough to make it through. Right now they may only be able to see the ragged underside of this tapestry, but believe me, they will come to appreciate the beauty that only the Lord can bring from this."

Everyone was so good here. Simcha's words really warmed my heart and comforted me. I knew my Lord would take care of my family. I couldn't imagine what they were going through with all the fear and torment in that sin-world. I was glad to forget about that place, but I loved my family so deeply. And my friends. Oh, how I loved my precious friends. A slow smile broke out on my face as a thought crossed my mind.

"I'll bet my passing will have a real impact on my friends, won't it?" I asked Simcha.

"It is already making a significant impact on many of their faith walks," he nodded in certainty.

"The gospel was shared at your funeral and impacted many of your friends, including Christians who were inspired to be more bold with their faith." He let that sink in for a few seconds and then continued stoically, "Further, there was a strong message about the dangers of drinking and driving that impacted your friends."

I absorbed this warm, happy thought that seemed to begin in my heart and then radiate through my being. I finally understood. God was going to turn everything out for good. That was the front of the tapestry! We always win. With Jesus, we always win.

Simcha smiled at me like a math teacher smiles when you've finally figured out a tricky calculus formula. I smiled back, amazed at the wisdom I was acquiring here.

"With Jesus, we always win..." I whispered, longing to hug Him again.

We sensed it together. It was as if the air carried His warm, familiar presence and we both smiled at each other. Jesus was on His way back, and in fact I knew intuitively He wasn't much further away than the tower He'd disappeared behind. I couldn't contain myself and jumped up and down squeeling. Then I took off in a mad dash to meet Him. I could hear Simcha laughing loudly behind me.

Chapter Seven:

To Be Continued

——∞∞∞——

I really dislike sad endings in movies, and before I even start to watch a movie I want to know whether it has a happy ending or not. My rationale is simple: if I know that I'll like the ending, it frees me to enjoy the movie. If I'm watching TV, I can change the channel if I don't like it. In life, however, we can't simply change the channel. I didn't like what the policeman's knock on the door did to the story of my life, and over and over it seemed like a bad movie with no ending. Fortunately, what helped me survive was the knowledge that ultimately, there would be a happy ending—eternal life in Heaven with Jesus.

One thing I have learned in this journey is that we undoubtedly live in a cosmic drama. The story of Job illustrates this. The story begins with Job being entirely unaware of the conversation occurring between God and Satan. God was praising Job on his exemplary life, while Satan claimed that Job loved God only because of what God had given him. Satan contended that Job would disown God if faced with trials. God took Satan up on his challenge and allowed him to test Job. As a result, Job was selected to undergo a staggering trial of faith. Consider that we also may be in the process of being tested. God wants us to trust Him and be faithful, just as Job was.

You are unaware of the unseen universe watching you. Perhaps a wager has been placed involving the testing of your faith. A cosmos of invisible beings, good and evil, may be observing you with intense interest. Powerful warriors battle one another, some for us, some against.[12]

I like the way Joni Erickson brings the scenario even closer to home. Can you imagine...

...angels sitting in the passenger seat of my car and getting an earful out of my outburst when that red Chevrolet cut me off? Demons wringing their hands in glee, hoping I'll curse at my kids when they cross me? Principalities and powers watching on tiptoe to see whether I turn to God or turn away?[13]

I personally want my Lord and the angels to rejoice at my behavior, and Satan to look at me with disgust. In this light, I like to think of the book of Job as a play. We in the audience get a sneak preview. We know the final act and want to tell Job, *Hang in there, Job, it's going to turn out okay! A* look behind the curtain gives us the big picture. We have an advantage that Job didn't have. We have the complete Word of God—the Bible. We have the end of the story, happy ending and all. As God began His healing work in me, He helped me see so clearly that my little life is part of a bigger story—a story with much broader and beautiful purposes than I have imagined. I had a choice whether to cooperate with His story, or to resist, as if to say: "I want to write my own story."

I am not suggesting that it's easy to accept God's will and obey Him in the wake of loss, even when we have this "inside information" that we ultimately win. When it hits close to home, and you lose something precious, your faith walk gets real.

My faith was tested the day the police report arrived in the mail. Initially, I didn't want to know any details about the accident, afraid that I would relive the accident over and over in my mind. However, a compulsion to know what happened overcame my need to protect myself from the details. If it had been a newspaper article, I would never have finished reading it. It wasn't an article, though; it was a detailed police report of my daughter's tragic accident. I sobbed uncontrollably as I read, my mind swirling with painful emotions and difficult questions. After I finished the last page, I fell to the floor and begged God for comfort. It took some time, but ultimately God spoke to my heart saying that this was not the last chapter of Danielle's life. This was the beginning of her story in Heaven!

To honor Danielle's birthday two years after she went home, I wrote this on her website:

> Our precious Danielle would have turned 22 today. A few days ago I was reading her journal and was crying as I thought, *Danielle's story was just beginning.* I then read a statement that she had written in her journal: My goal is to fix my eyes on Jesus and be His follower.
>
> Even though I had read this goal a number of times, it affected me in a different way. She's still living out this goal! C.S. Lewis illustrates this well in *The Last Battle*:
>
> > But for them it was only the beginning of the real story. All their life in this world and all their adventures in Narnia had only been the cover and the title page: now at last they were beginning Chapter One of the Great Story, which no one on earth has read: which goes on forever: in which every chapter is better than the one before.[14]
>
> I draw strength from this truth every day. For a Christian, death is not the end of life, but a continuation of it in Heaven.

As I rounded the tower, Jesus was walking toward me already smiling. He laughed and held His arms open wide as I ran full speed into them. He picked me up off of my feet at the last millisecond and spun me around. Then he set me down and looked at me with a sort of fatherly gaze for a second.

"You've been having fun?" He asked, still beaming.

"Oh yes!" I said, "Simcha has been explaining a lot to me."

"It's making sense?" He asked, raising His eyebrows to make sure.

"Overall yes, my Lord." It's difficult to explain the love and reverence you experience in His presence, but it is His approachability that blew me away. I was standing before the King of Kings, but He genuinely cared for me.

"Good," He answered. He put His arm around my shoulder and drew me close to Him. "You will understand more in time."

My entourage had now caught up to us, as had Simcha, and they all thronged around us. Jesus was simply magnetic.

As soon as everyone was near, He started walking toward the city. I linked my arm in His, still looking up at His face. He leaned down to me and said quietly, "I have a surprise for you!" Instantly I felt like a little girl on Christmas morning.

"Really? What is it?" I asked the obvious.

"Well, it wouldn't be much of a surprise if I told you, would it?" He chuckled.

"Oh, Lord Jesus, you know how much I hate suspense!" I tugged on His arm.

He laughed again and said, "Ah, indeed I do." He paused with a mischievous grin. "But I also know you have memorized the fruit of the spirit."

I stopped and gave Him a "Seriously?" look, knowing immediately He was talking about the virtue of patience. He laughed again, but still wouldn't tell me.

"Come!" He said, waving me on. "It's worth waiting for."

I sighed dramatically and then ran quickly to catch up with Him. He looked down at me with a twinkle in His eye and a wave of love overwhelmed me again.

I smiled to myself. I was in *Heaven*!

"Lord?" I asked Him as we walked arm in arm again.

"Yes, my love?"

"Is there anything I can do to make sure my family and friends are guaranteed to be here with me?"

He paused for a second and then said gently, "Danielle, you did a lot in your short time on earth."

"Thank You, Lord Jesus," I answered, my entire being rippling with His words of praise. "I just wondered if there is anything I can do *now*?"

"My dear child," He began. "Your time of proving and refinement is over. You have entered into My rest now, but I know you are still very concerned about those who were closest to you on earth."

I listened intently. His words carried a reassurance that seemed to carry a healing balm.

"Rest assured, my darling, that I have planned in detail for every eventuality, and I am consistently interceding for those who have not yet completed their race before our Father."

Something caught my attention.

"What sort of details did you plan for?" I asked.

"All *kinds* of details," He said with a smile and the air of a humble, yet master engineer.

"Well, can you tell me one from my life?"

He nodded. "There is actually a very special one just before you ended your journey on earth."

We had passed the big tower and now rounded a corner that led into a street at the beginning of the city. It was simply breathtaking. I was going to prompt Him further, but paused to take in the site of the most beautiful architecture continuing down the street as far as I could see. I was no expert but the various styles were so different yet not disparate. They flowed organically and flawlessly from one building to the next. In a way I've never known before, I knew these astounding buildings reflected their occupants perfectly. The gardens, trees, and flowerbeds exhibited almost too much art and beauty to take in all at once. I knew He had created these mansions for other believers. I almost fell on my knees again at the realization of the infinite genius and majesty in Whose presence I felt barely worthy to stand. He caught my arm with His again before I could, and I just swallowed hard, looking up at Him in awe. He continued our conversation as we kept walking.

"Do you remember feeling very compelled to do something in the week before you left earth?" He asked, as though He had no idea I was still feeling giddy from being in the presence of *the* Master Craftsman.

"Uhh, compelled..?" I focused, and then it came to me. I really wanted some of my friends to have words of love and encouragement and took time to write these messages. "The cards," I said looking up to Him for confirmation. "The cards I wrote out?"

He nodded. "Yes, the cards."

"I never got the chance to send them." I hadn't realized this until now and my heart suddenly sank.

"Do you believe anything my children do goes unnoticed by Me?"

"No, Lord, of course not," I answered. After the wonders I'd experienced so far, at the hand of my Creator, I knew it was impossible for Him to miss anything.

"Well, do you remember what I said earlier about the seeds of a ministry being planted within your mom?"

"Yes!" I nodded vigorously. The thought filled me with such joy.

"Those cards are some of the seeds of that ministry, Danielle." He smiled.

Yet again, I was flooded with so many wonderful emotions—joy, relief, love, worship. It seemed around every corner there was fulfillment, security, and wonder in my new home. And it all came from one Source: my Lord and Savior.

"My Lord, Your words never cease to encourage me," I said. Like the last time, I felt an overwhelming urge to bow before Him. This time I followed my heart.

I dropped to my knees and bowed my head, and said a phrase that bubbled up out of me like a river: "Praise be to the great God, Jehovah!"

"Praise be to the great God, Jehovah!" my family and Simcha roared in unison. As I worshiped, I heard the most beautiful sound I had ever heard. Bells and chimes and stringed instruments sang a melody so complex, but so astoundingly gorgeous.

I looked up and was almost startled by the sight. Jesus was shining brightly, and all around us citizens were standing on their balconies, or in the street, and worshiping in perfect harmony. Beyond that, angels hovered all around, both near and far off, joining in on this impromptu melodic adoration of our majestic God. The waves of what I can only describe as glory still flowed as I watched, enthralled. I forgot about all my questions, all of my ponderings, and seemed to soar into an entirely new realm through the worship. It was pure glory.

Nathan and I were watching an old rerun of *MacGyver*, and because we have the series on DVD, I've noticed a pattern. There's always a villain, a hero (MacGyver), and always a happy ending where the good guys win. There was one episode, however, where I didn't like the ending. The villain was winning...and it ended.

What? I thought. *It can't end here!* (Remember how much I hate sad endings?) Then three important words appeared on the screen: *To be continued.* It hit me—in the story of my life I had experienced a situation that looked incredibly hopeless, and I certainly couldn't imagine how there could be a happy ending. Similar to the story on television, however, it only appeared like it was over, and God continues to show me ever-expanding pieces of the story that give me hope. The primary concept that has been so important in my healing is this: I cannot lose sight of the bigger picture—that bigger picture is eternal life in Heaven.

There have been chapters in my life story that I have not liked, and I would have wanted to re-write. I'm part of a greater story directed by God and I need to trust Him. There will be happy moments written into the continuing script of my life, but I'm sure there will also be scenes that will break my heart. Someday, in the presence of Christ, I will have the benefit of retrospect. I will be able to look back and see the full story. I will see how all things really did work together for good.

In November of 2008, on Danielle's website, I wrote a letter to those who were hurting and ended with these words:

> Throughout Danielle's life, she embarked on several journeys—when she took her first hesitant steps as a baby, her first day of kindergarten, her excitement as she started high school, her first day at college. Danielle has begun the most beautiful, magnificent, and rewarding journey of all, in her eternal, heavenly home!
>
> I always imagined helping her plan her wedding, watching her walk down the aisle to meet her groom. Well—Danielle is now with her "heavenly bridegroom" Whom she has loved ever since she gave her heart to Him as a precious little girl. Whenever I feel that intense pain of missing her, I remind myself that my separation from Danielle is temporary. When God is finished with me here, I'll be welcomed by Jesus, my dad, and Danielle shouting, "Welcome home, Mom." What a celebration that will be!

Chapter Eight:

ETERNAL PERSPECTIVE

---✗✗✗---

M any years ago our family went to Disney World. A favorite show for me was, *Honey I Shrunk The Audience*, and the key to the show were the 3-D glasses. When you wore the glasses, you saw things differently. This principle has been true in my grief journey as well. I needed a new set of lenses to help me see life differently. Looking at life through God's eyes gave me an eternal perspective.

I have been asked what has been the most significant influence on me during my grief journey. There is no doubt in my mind, having an eternal perspective has been the crucial factor in my healing. Even during the first year when the grief was so very hard, God gave me hope that came from knowing that this life I am experiencing is not all there is. John 11:25-26 speaks directly to this comfort: "Jesus told her, 'I am the resurrection and the life. Those who believe in me, even though they die like everyone else, will live again. They are given eternal life for believing in me and will never perish.'" (NLT)

What's more, asking God to help me to live in light of eternity has changed my focus, but also my perspective on verses such as Philippians 3:20, which states: "But our citizenship is in Heaven. And we eagerly await a Savior from there, the Lord Jesus Christ." Before Danielle's accident, Heaven was something I definitely believed in, but I didn't think about it often. After the accident, however, Heaven became an infinite source of comfort.

During this time I talked to a friend who couldn't appreciate why I had such an insatiable desire to understand and think about Heaven so much. I asked her to imagine her daughter studying abroad in Zambia, Africa for a year. She would *Google* Zambia and devour every piece of information she could find because her daughter was going to be living there. Well, that's how I felt—Danielle was living in Heaven and I wanted to understand what it was like for her there.

I went through a tough time many years ago, and during that trial in my life I had a very vivid dream. My manager offered me an opportunity; I would be given an assignment that would last a week. It would be the most incredibly stressful, horrible week—performing tasks that were significantly beyond my comfort zone. Most of the other employees would despise me and do whatever they could to make my life miserable. But after one week I would be promoted, given my ideal job, ideal location, ideal co-workers, and work just a few hours a week.

So the question from my manager was, "Do you want to take on this opportunity?" Well, of course I would. I woke up and thought, *"what a strange dream,"* but later reflected on it and saw similarities to God's plan for His children. Yes, we will experience trials and suffering on this earth, but our life here on this earth is a minuscule fraction of our time in eternity, where we will live in paradise completely devoid of the pain we now endure.

When we experience hardship, it is critical to have a vision that keeps us from being swept away by discouragement. My vision includes eternal life with Jesus. Many people suffering loss experience hopelessness when they tell themselves that this life we have here is all there is.

When I look back many years ago to a time when I was struggling, I realize now that God was building an eternal perspective in my life that could carry me through the toughest times. This included the horrific storm that devastated my world when Danielle died. It was important for me to be established in my faith before the crisis hit, even though my faith has certainly grown during this season. My journal from that season long ago records insight that is helping me in this new season. It reads, "It is important to understand the brevity of life, realizing that we are just passing through...on our way to our final destination."

Do you remember the movie, *Apollo 13*—about the mission to the moon and the challenge to bring the astronauts home safely? I loved the ending. People all over the world sat transfixed, with their eyes glued to their television screens wondering if the astronauts would arrive safely. And then, suddenly, the capsule appears. The words from home were, "Odyssey, Houston, welcome home! We're glad to see you." Cheers went up from all over the world for their safe arrival. I find it is a fitting analogy of Danielle's journey through life, through the horrible accident, and then finally her homecoming where she was welcomed home to Heaven by cheers and applause.

If I focused on the loss of Danielle from a human perspective, life would be unbearable. The truth is, however, I had to make the choice to see the accident as God sees it, that Danielle is safely home. Yes, from my earthly perspective Danielle's life was way too brief, but in comparison to eternity, no one has a long life. Our days here on earth are like a drop in the ocean.

One day as I was browsing through old photo albums, I found pictures of the girls on the beach. This reminded me of a story that took place on the way home from that vacation. I was at the airport with Ashley (who was two months old) and Danielle (who was two-and-a-half years old). My curious, adventuresome Danielle decided to go exploring—without her mom. I soon realized Danielle wasn't with me, and as you can imagine, I panicked. Holding Ashley and trying to maneuver our luggage, I anxiously searched for my little Amelia Earhart. Thankfully, I found her nearby. Breathing a sigh of relief I managed to get to the other side of the airport and we found our gate.

Of course when we arrived, I was told there had been a gate change. I would have to trek back to the other side of the airport. I was entirely stressed and completely distraught, but we tried to remain cheerful as we chugged along. When we finally got back to where we started, I realized we had left Danielle's precious monkey, Freddie, behind. Parents know this is a catastrophic situation. You just don't find another monkey and pass it off as Freddie. Freddie had to be rescued—and fast. Danielle started crying, which soon led to Ashley screaming. I was so stressed I was visibly shaking and not even close to thinking clearly. I carried my, now two, screaming kids to someone who looked official, and in a voice that probably sounded hysterical, I cried, "We lost Freddie!"

The gentleman patiently asked, "How old is Freddie?"

"Two," I replied, as I calculated that Danielle had acquired Freddie when she was still a baby.

Within moments, an eager band of authorities were summoned to launch an urgent hunt (thinking, of course, they were searching for a vulnerable, two-year-old little boy).

"What does he look like?" one of them asked me.

"He's wearing a blue cap," I replied, as both kids started crying more loudly. Ashley's face was getting red, which made me even more panicky, and with my voice rising in pitch and volume, I added, "and part of his right leg is chewed off."

At that point everyone within twenty-five feet stopped in their tracks and stared at me.

Sensing I was close to a complete breakdown, a dear elderly lady came up and offered to help me with Ashley. This gave me the opportunity to explain that Freddie was, in fact, not a two-year-old boy, but was our two-year-old stuffed monkey. After a few grumbles and disgruntled murmurs, we got Freddie back!

I'd like to share that the remainder of our trip home was uneventful, but unfortunately Ashley had an ear infection, so I spent the majority of the entire flight walking up and down the aisle with an unhappy little girl. Danielle waited patiently, and as we were leaving she looked at me with sad eyes. I realized shortly after that with mom being preoccupied, she didn't quite make it to the bathroom in time. I gave her that reassuring smile that everything would be fine and did what any responsible mom would do: put the blue airport blanket over the wet spot and walked out. I can't tell you how great our home looked when we walked in that evening!

The story illustrates an important concept. My trip home may have been stressful, but the airplane was not my destination—I was heading home to Minnesota. Similarly, this life is not our final destination. This truth offers hope, not just in the future, but right now, in the midst of our trials. We live in a world where trials will enter our lives, and if all of our hope rests on this life, we will experience despair and hopelessness. The hope of eternal life can radically change how we approach trials in our lives.

I'm so thankful that I kept notes and cards Danielle had sent me because they have been a blessing to me. In the weeks following the accident, I found one card Danielle had given me in high school. She was dealing with some hurts related to a friend, and I told her I was praying for her. There were two sentences in her card that captured my heart, "Thanks mom for praying. Someday I'll be in Heaven and I won't have to deal with this stuff anymore."

Tears came flooding as I pondered that when Danielle had written this, neither she nor I would ever have imagined that she would be in Heaven so soon. But she was right. She no longer had to deal with "this stuff" anymore. After reading this note, I found myself ruminating about my loss, which was making me feel worse. I described in my journal what helped me to move out of this funk:

> I received an email from a friend who included Romans 8:18 in her message, "I consider that our present sufferings are not worth comparing with the glory that will be revealed in us." I subsequently wrote this in my journal: Because I live with the assurance of eternal life, nothing that happens to me

can be really debilitating as there is no comparison between trials in this life and what I will experience in Heaven.

Another passage of scripture that has been a gift from God is 2 Corinthians 4:16-18: "Therefore we do not lose heart. Though outwardly we are wasting away, yet inwardly we are being renewed day by day. For our light and momentary troubles are achieving for us an eternal glory that far outweighs them all. So we fix our eyes not on what is seen, but on what is unseen, since what is seen is temporary, but what is unseen is eternal."

Paul had every reason to lose heart, having suffered incredible persecution. He states that our faithfulness while experiencing trials results in eternal glory. This is so powerful when it sinks in. I heard a pastor explain this scripture using the following analogy. When you feel the heavy weight of troubles, imagine a scale. Place your troubles on one side of the scale and your eternal rewards on the other. The rewards side will crash down as eternity spent with your Savior far outweighs any pain being experienced now. Holding on to this perspective when we suffer hardships will ease the pain.

Most of us do not see beyond the horizons of this world. If we embrace this verse, we will understand that this present life is but a brief window of opportunity to invest in what will last for eternity. Now does that mean I'm at the point where I say, "Bring on those trials because I'm focusing on my eternal glory"? No. Remember, we are all a work in progress and God is clearly not through with me yet.

I remember the day Danielle came home from school and she told me about an illustration her teacher had used. There was a very long piece of string wrapped around the room multiple times and a small dot on the string. The dot represents our whole life here on earth. For Danielle that was twenty years. The long string represents our life after death in eternity. The Bible clearly shows that what happens inside the dot will affect our heavenly rewards forever. God notices our character, faithfulness, and our every attempt to serve Him. Another powerful reminder that we have a choice to live for what we can see, the tiny dot on the string, or we can live for eternity.

My prayer would be for you to truly grasp the concept of the brevity of life. When you begin to see Heaven as your true home, you can develop an eternal perspective that sees all sorrows as fleeting. As I've discussed in previous chapters, God's story reminds us that no matter how dark the chapter you're living in, or how final things feel, in Christ there is always another chapter. A continued story that is ultimately victorious.

DANIELLE'S SMILE COULD
LIGHT UP A ROOM!

Danielle's little buddy, Nathan

Even in Arizona, as a student at Grand Canyon University,
Danielle found time to snowboard.

Danielle loved the beach.

Danielle spent the day with Ashley helping her get ready for the party— Ashley's prom. Two weeks later Danielle attended a far greater party—her *homecoming party!*

Chapter Nine:

Every Reason To Hope

---⸎---

I counsel many people who feel hopeless for a variety of reasons. It is an awful feeling since hope is essential for us to make it through life. Hope enables us to hold on and not give in to despair, even when the circumstances around us look bleak.

This chapter carries really good news. You can regain hope—the hope that restores your soul as you move into His joy and peace. When biblical writers used the word "hope," they did not intend the ascribed meaning that has become so common today, namely "wishing something were a certain way." The biblical concept of hope is one of assurance and complete trust. Biblical hope carries connotations of victory over this world and over death, because Jesus has conquered both.

I have learned that the things we place our hope in will influence the way we respond to life. Most of what we put our hope in will eventually fail us. We often evaluate our lives based on circumstances, people in our lives, and possessions, and losing them can lead to feelings of hopelessness. When our security is in Christ, and we factor in eternity, we have an unshakeable reason for hope.

That being said, I found that when I felt discouraged, I could lose my perspective. I remember one day I went into

Danielle's room and was looking through one of her photo albums. I so desperately wanted a hug from her, to see her big smile and to hear her laugh. I expressed my pain in my journal as I wrote, "I'm not sure if I can walk down this road—many things remind me of Danielle. God, will the pain end?" Shortly after writing this, I received an email from my dear friend, Sandy. In the email, she told me how she and her daughter were driving one early evening and came upon the stretch of road where Danielle's accident had taken place. She then described what they saw.

In the sky directly above the accident location, there was an opening in the clouds with the sun's rays beaming down through the gap. Her daughter took a picture, and later as they looked at the photo they could see twenty rays of light (Danielle's age) shining through the clouds. She also pointed out that the shape of the white space in the middle of the clouds looked like an outline of Jesus' head and shoulders.

She emailed me the picture and it gave me a new perspective that felt like those beams of light piercing a dark sky of despair in my heart. I clearly needed a "hope transplant," and I don't think it was a coincidence that I received the picture at that time. It was my postcard from Heaven and it lifted my spirits.

My friend, Gayle, battled cancer for many years until she finally went to her eternal home in Heaven. Her attitude throughout the entire ordeal remained positive and communicated tremendous hope to others. Gayle's gracious and generous spirit was embodied in her refusal to live in bitterness, and it visibly affected everyone she encountered. She had complete faith that God could heal her, but realized physical healing may not be God's decision. Her love for God never wavered even when the diagnosis looked bleak. There were times when I thought, *God, why? You have unlimited power and can so easily heal her.* Gayle, however, strongly believed that her suffering was a part of God's redemptive purpose in some way. She was a living witness of the power of God, and blessed and inspired many people through her suffering. I have learned that situations don't have to turn out my way for them to turn out for good in the kingdom of God.

When Gayle passed away, this poem was read at her funeral, and I think beautifully illustrates why Christians have hope:

Gone From My Sight

I am standing upon a seashore. A ship at my side spreads her white sails to the morning breeze and starts for the blue ocean. She is an object of beauty and strength. I stand and watch her until at length she hangs like a speck of white cloud just where the sea and sky come to mingle with each other.

Then someone at my side says: "There, she is gone!" "Gone where?"

Gone from my sight. That is all. She is just as large in mast and hull and spar as she was when she left my side and she is just as able to bear the load of living freight to her destined port. Her diminished size is in me, not in her. And just at the moment when someone at my side says: "There, she is gone!" There are other eyes watching her coming, and other voices ready to take up the glad shout "HERE SHE COMES!"

And that is dying

— Henry Van Dyke

This poem illustrates that Danielle and our loved ones who know the Lord merely move from Earth to Heaven. We are having our painful, tearful goodbyes, while Jesus and others welcome them home.

I experienced such joy whenever I sensed that Ashley and Nathan grasped the truth that despite the grief, we could have hope for an awesome future. I walked into the kitchen one day and Ashley and Nathan were imagining the home that Danielle and the two of them would live in some day. It was precious hearing them describe in detail what they envisioned. I asked if I could live there as well, and Nathan replied, "No, but you can live two houses down from us." That response was given when he was eleven; now that he's seventeen, he may want a few more miles between the homes.

As I close this chapter, just think about how comforting it is to know our pain is temporary, yet the joy we will experience in Heaven is eternal. That is a truth that brings real hope!

———— ∞ ————

We had reached a sort of subdivision with absolutely beautiful houses on huge tracts of land. I really liked the look of one house on the left of the road. It was a sprawling, double-story house with what looked like a swimming area on the side. The architecture was just amazing.

"Whoa!" I said. "Check out that house! That place is *sweet!*"

Jesus smiled at me. "You like that one?" Suddenly I realized what the surprise was.

"No way!" I gasped. "Lord Jesus!" I said shyly. "Is that my MANSION?" I started jumping up and down.

"Whoa, whoa, whoa!" He said, raising His hand. "Danielle, that's not your mansion." He looked serious.

"Stop kidding around, Lord. This place is so cool! This is the surprise, right?"

He shook His head solemnly.

"Hmm," I said, a little confused. It really felt like it was my house. It just had a certain home-quality to it.

"THAT'S your home," He said suddenly, pointing to a gigantic house on the next, massive parcel of land. I looked at Him and He grinned from ear to ear, and nodded. He looked *so* excited. I looked at the house in the distance and started to notice similar features to this one and more. I realized the house backed up to a huge mountain covered in snow. My jaw must have been hanging open as Jesus gently pushed my chin up to close my mouth. I swallowed and looked at Him. The joy in His eyes was unexplainable.

"Well, c'mon. Let's go see it!" He grabbed my hand and pulled me along the road.

I didn't need a second invitation. We both started sprinting toward the manor, laughing. Within minutes we were at the edge of the land. I stopped and put my hand over my mouth. I surveyed the most astounding piece of architecture I had ever laid eyes on. It was similar to the first house but this one was simply perfect. It was two stories in most places, and three in some. The angles, heights, and roofs over each section all formed complimentary patterns. This house also had ornate gables, but in a much more modern fashion. Flowering gardens and rockeries spread out across the front landscape, and there was a huge swimming pool to the front-right corner. A water slide curved through a multilayered, waterfall garden. This house embodied everything I had ever dreamed of.

The crowning achievement, however, loomed behind the house. The colossal peak of a majestic mountain was covered in what looked like pure powder—the softest, most perfect kind of snow for snowboarding. The mountainside was filled with steeps and bumps, and picturesque trees and shrubs lined the paths neatly.

"Oh, my Lord." I buried my head in His shoulder. "It's too beautiful for words!" If tears were able to flow freely in Heaven, I would have been sobbing with joy. Instead, I just squeezed Him for all I was worth.

Eventually He gently put His hands on my shoulders and held me at arm's length. He looked deeply into my eyes with what I can only describe as infinite love and simply said, "I love you Danielle."

I was instantly overwhelmed and plunged my head into His shoulder again. "Thank You!" I whispered. "Thank You. I love it. I love everything about the house. I love YOU!"

He returned my squeeze as He chuckled in delight. I could tell this was wonderful for Him.

After a while, I withdrew my head from against His strong shoulder and looked at the house. Every detail had my personality perfectly embodied in this house. It had a sort of designer log-home feel to it in one way, and a masterpiece of modern architecture in another. It was all Danielle.

"It has an inside too!" Jesus grinned at me. I could only sigh again, overcome with emotion. He laughed. I could tell my reaction was the best reward He could ever have. But I would spend eternity being grateful and in total love with my Savior. Not even my family knew me this well.

"Lord?" I had a question, before I went exploring.

"Yes, Danielle."

"Why did I think that other house was mine at first?"

"That house felt very much like it was meant for you, didn't it?" He replied softly.

"Yes, it really did. I would have been happy in that house. It looked so comfortable. Yet..."

"Not entirely you." He completed my train of thought. "That house is for someone who is similar to you, my dear. That's why it felt so comfortable. It had a *home* quality to it as well."

"Well whose house is that?" I wasn't getting anxious, but I knew I wanted my loved ones to finish their work on earth.

"Don't be concerned, my child," He smiled in full reassurance. "Only the outside of that house appears complete. I am still preparing the inside and aspects of the outside. I still have plenty of time to work on that one and the others around both of these houses."

I broke into a smile that was huge, even for me. Someday I would help Jesus surprise my family with their estates, just like He had surprised me. But it wouldn't be for a while. I had a feeling there would be enough to keep me occupied until then.

Suddenly I saw movement inside the front room.

"Hey! Who is in my house?" I squawked.

The front door slowly opened, and standing there was the majestic angel, Simcha. He was holding a tray of glasses full of what looked like lemonade or some delicious beverage. I could feel his radiant smile from the front lawn. I waved, and he bowed his head slightly in greeting. I realized his hands were full and giggled.

"Oh, Lord Jesus," I said again. "This house is so beautiful. You really *know* me!"

Jesus smiled at me with those unexplainable, loving eyes and looked at me like I wasn't getting an inside joke.

"Sooo, it has an inside *too*," Jesus repeated, nudging me and clearly getting antsy to show me something inside.

"Oh, I'm sure it's perfect inside." I grinned at Him, but I clearly wasn't picking up on what He was trying to say.

"What sort of room have you always wanted in a house?" He asked me, obviously not able to wait any more.

"Huh? I don't know...A big bedr..." Then it struck me. The mountain. The snow. Suddenly it all made sense.

"A room full of SNOWBOARD GEAR?" I yelled, unable to control myself.

"AHA!" Jesus replied, just as loud. I was jumping up and down now and He laughed as He grabbed my hands and started jumping too. (I remember on earth, that it might have seemed like a disrespectful image of our Lord, but believe me...He *jumps* for joy!)

"Come and SEE!" He shouted and took off toward the house. I was laughing hysterically because He was almost more excited than me, but I bolted madly after Him. I still couldn't get used to how everything just kept getting better and better in Heaven. If I knew my Lord, these would be some supernatural snowboards! For a moment I thought of my family. If only they knew of the hope that lay before them. They wouldn't be sad for an instant. I smiled as I thought, *The Holy Spirit is on top of that. He'll make sure they know!* I broke into a full sprint, as I couldn't let Jesus beat me to the snowboard room.

Chapter Ten:

HOLIDAYS AND SPECIAL DATES

———— ∞∞∞ ————

W hen you've lost a loved one, there are dates, places, and events that can be painful reminders of your loss. This was certainly true for me. Special dates triggered an intense longing for my girl. This pain became less intense over time, but the waves of grief do still continue and may for many years.

Holidays can especially be painful and difficult, and emotions can suddenly become raw again. There has been no easy solution for the sadness that surfaces around the holidays. However, I have found that volunteering or reaching out to others in need relieves some of this pain. Traditions also remind us of our loss, so adding a new tradition or changing past ones helps. Being open to others about what we need during the holidays has also been very important.

Our last Christmas with Danielle had some especially memorable moments. It was a difficult Christmas for me, since it was the first without my dad. Danielle and I were talking about how we could help the family enjoy it, regardless. Dad was known as "The Encourager," and truly provided joy to everyone he met. Danielle came up with the idea to capture that spirit by printing "JOY" in gold letters on small, polished rocks and presenting them to the entire family on Christmas Eve. It went over so well, and was such a precious gesture of love, especially to my mom. I remember Danielle just beaming as she saw how much it meant to everyone to get their "Joy rocks." Little did we know that five months later, Danielle, also a renowned encourager and joy-giver, would be ushered into the very presence of the Lord she loved so much, joining her Grandpa.

As the first Christmas holiday without Danielle was approaching, I thought of ways to ease the grief a little. I planned a time where our family could reminisce over memories of her, reflecting on all of the joy Danielle brought to our life and imagining what she was doing in Heaven. I wrote some of these memories in my journal, including Nathan's hope to someday go snowboarding with Danielle in Heaven. "And," he added, "I won't need to wear a helmet in Heaven!"

I posted this to the website the first Christmas:

> Our first Christmas without our precious Danielle. Oh how we miss her! As I reflect on previous Christmases, I have a memory of a time when Danielle was 4 years old. Danielle loved manger scenes and there was one in particular where baby Jesus looked so real. I remember her staring intently at the face, and then leaning over to gently touch the face of baby Jesus. Danielle is no longer looking at a manger scene made by humans; she's with Jesus and can lean over and touch His face. Christmas in Heaven. I simply can't imagine the beauty Danielle is experiencing!

> I know there are many who will be saying, "Merry Christmas" to others, but inside they may be hurting and will need encouragement at this time of year. The essential message of Christmas is, "Immanuel—God is with you." God will help you and strengthen you. I pray that you will feel God's presence and love during this season.

For me personally, Mother's Day is the most emotional holiday. This could be because the last time I saw Danielle was Mother's Day 2008. Now, every Mother's Day, after the day's activities are done, I retrieve Danielle's letter from my drawer to read. I always end up crying as my heart just aches to be with her.

On the evening of my first Mother's Day without Danielle, as I sat there in a flood of tears reading her letter, I was surprised to hear the doorbell ring. Curious, I went to the front door and was even more pleasantly surprised when two of Danielle's friends walked in bearing flowers for me. What a precious gift.

After losing a loved one, it is important to understand that deep pain and intense emotions can surface at unique moments. You may be doing fine, when out of nowhere comes an agonizing ambush, where you feel intense sadness, rage, or other feelings. In time you may become aware of the places or events that trigger this response, but even then, often the intensity of the emotions are unexpected.

As I have learned, however, some ambushes you can simply never prepare for. One evening, just after I had dropped Nathan off at youth group, I received a call on my cell phone. It was a good friend of mine and her tone of voice indicated this wasn't a call to chat. She wanted to make me aware that Danielle's car was on display outside of Culvers restaurant, less than two miles from the church. Initially I couldn't respond, feeling that ache in my stomach start up again. She offered to meet me there, but I had never seen the car and wasn't sure I could handle it emotionally. I started to drive home, but then for some reason, found myself turning around and heading toward Culvers, despite an awful sense of dread.

I pulled into the parking lot and saw the MADD trailer with Danielle's crumpled, red car on it. Three large metal billboards were attached to the trailer; two with pictures of Danielle and the other, her story. I was already becoming emotionally overwhelmed, watching people read the story and peer into the car. I waited for them to leave and walked over, my tears now streaming as I approached the car. I was visibly shaking by the time I stepped onto the trailer and peered inside. On the passenger seat was a John 3:16 booklet by Max Lucado and a Stacy Orrico DVD. I picked up the booklet and felt a sense of supernatural relief. I said a quick prayer thanking God that Danielle believed in Him.

That night, I prayed for wisdom in deciding whether I should bring Nathan to view the car. I pulled out Randy Alcorn's book called *Tell Me about Heaven*[15], which I had previously read to Nathan. I sat down with him once more so that together we could look at the section called, *The Voyage Home*. The book uses Luke 16:22 to talk about how, in the story, Jake's grandma was taken to Heaven: "The time came when the beggar died and the angels carried him to Abraham's side."

I read the passage to prepare Nathan to see the car, and the next day he and I drove to Culvers. When we were driving, I glanced over and he looked so sad, which just broke my heart. As we approached the car, I reminded him that this was where God reached down and angels escorted Danielle to Heaven. I felt such a sense of loss and helplessness seeing the tears roll down Nathan's cheeks and the intense grief in his eyes as he stared at Danielle's beautiful face displayed on the car.

As Nathan and I were driving home, we were tuned to KTIS, (our local Christian radio station) and God gave us a gift. Chris Rice's song called "Come to Jesus" came on. We had played this ballad as a backdrop to one of the videos at the funeral. By the end of it I was crying, but also feeling God comfort me, as I realized I was right at the location where Danielle did "fly to Jesus and live!"

The anniversary of Danielle's death triggers a deep longing to have her back. Traditionally, I go to the cemetery with family, and I try to make it as special as possible. On the second anniversary of Danielle's home-going, a friend came along. What could have been a difficult memory for me is now a joyful one, as we laid out blankets and shared Danielle stories while we ate tasty snacks and drank "pink" lemonade (a tribute to Danielle's favorite color).

Birthdays can be a time where the loss feels fresh. A family tradition was to have a "blessing" for each of the children on their birthday. This included a special dinner, which was a time for everyone to share what they love about the person, and a blessing letter. The letter included all of the highlights of the previous year, special photos, and a verse for the person. I found it helped me to create a letter for Danielle on the day that she would have turned twenty-one. Below are two paragraphs from her twenty-first birthday blessing letter.

> My dearest Danielle,
>
> I wrote these exact words a year ago in your blessing that I gave you on your twentieth birthday. "A sad moment this past year was saying goodbye to your grandpa, but knowing you'll see him again as he welcomes you at the heavenly gates with his booming voice exclaiming, 'Welcome Home, Danielle Joy.' I remember driving you to Bethel following his funeral. In tears you shared how you were influenced by the sharing time at the funeral. Realizing that Grandpa had made such an impact on so many lives, you told me that you want to have that type of impact on others, and that you wanted to be more bold in sharing your faith. I'm sure you will!"
>
> Danielle, sadly, you were welcomed home by Grandpa much sooner than anyone wanted. You have had an impact on so many people during your twenty years here, and your legacy continues...

Losing a child often results in many triggering events as a parent often "grows up with the loss," marking the times when the child would have graduated from high school, college, gotten married, and so on. There were times when a friend would be sharing their excitement over events in their child's life, such as a graduation, wedding, or pregnancy. I would be happy for them, but I also felt some sadness, as I would never share these experiences with Danielle.

Weddings can be particularly difficult if you are mourning the loss of a spouse or child. After losing Danielle, I attended the wedding of Matt and Angie, who were two of Danielle's close friends. It was a lovely, although very emotional event, as the groom and his brother were both pallbearers at Danielle's funeral. The wedding ceremony was in our church, so I watched the groom and his brother walk down the same aisle that they had walked down earlier, carrying Danielle's casket. All of these emotions were compounded upon my thoughts of how Danielle's wedding would have been.

A year later I experienced another wedding that triggered significant emotions. The ceremony was held at Northwestern College, where I attended for one year. The familiar chapel is a beautiful place for a wedding, and I had always wanted my girls to get married there. I walked into the chapel and tried my best to fight back the tears. I spent the next fifteen minutes walking the halls, hoping the tears would stop. I eventually realized I wasn't going to make it through the ceremony, so I went outside and found a bench overlooking the lake. The gorgeous day was a stark contrast between the songs of twittering, happy birds filling the air and my cries and earnest prayers, reminding God how very much it hurt, knowing I would never see my precious Danielle walking down the aisle at her wedding. I wept as I imagined how beautiful she would have looked in her wedding dress, with her radiant smile lighting up the chapel. I protested before God, *It's not fair! I want her back so very much.* Overwhelmed, I hunched over, crying so hard my whole body was shaking.

Just when I thought I couldn't take any more, I heard a song playing in the distance. It was soft and muffled, but I instantly recognized it. The unmistakable melody of "Blessed Be Your Name" drifted on the air toward this grief-stricken mom, crying alone next to a lake. The same praise chorus we sang at Danielle's funeral.

God did not always intervene in such a tangible way when I cried out to Him for comfort. Sometimes it was an email from a friend, sometimes a song or a verse, and sometimes it was pure faith that He would always be there for me even when I didn't feel it. Today, however, as I listened to the words of this beautiful song, I felt the intensity of pain's grip weaken, as if Jesus was wrapping His arms around me, showing me that even when the darkness closes in, He will never leave me. Praise Him forever!

I could hardly believe my eyes. Hanging on custom racks were probably twenty different snowboards, with varying shapes, tails, noses and graphics. I could tell each one was designed for a unique section of the mountain. And the graphics! The graphics were just mind-blowing. My favorite was a board that had a swirling galaxy on the bottom, containing stars and planets that shone with colors I had never seen before.

Simcha had opened the door for us and stood a little behind us with his hands folded behind his back. Jesus was loving the joy I displayed in His gifts to me. Simcha had a twinkle in his eyes, too.

"Come up here, Simcha!" I waved him forward. I didn't like this whole 'standing-behind-us' thing. "Tell me which board to try first."

"Ah well..." he began thoughtfully. "For the universe in your smile, dear Danielle, it would have to be the Galaxia design."

"The *Galaxia design*?" I squealed. "That's what you call it?" I looked at Jesus and He laughed, nodding. "That's the coolest thing I've ever heard!"

Simcha laughed now too and it was clear they were just enthralled I was so happy.

"Let's go! Lord...Simcha...grab a board!" I picked up the Galaxia. Oh, it was gorgeous.

"I won't be able to go with you, Danielle," Jesus said sweetly. "I have some things to prepare, but I've heard your friend Simcha here is quite the master of the alley-oop McTwist."

"WHAT?" I laughed. "No way!"

"Yes way," Jesus said, and looked over at Simcha. Simcha opened his palms and bowed slightly as if to say, *What can I say? It's true.*

"Aw, this I *have* to see!" I laughed again. "Grab a board!" I half-yelled to Simcha. "Let's go snowboarding!" The angel didn't have to be asked again.

We snowboarded for what seemed like the entire day! The runs were absolutely perfect. Jumps and rails and steeps and even a perfect half-pipe, naturally (and conveniently) fashioned between two cliffs. I was pulling off tricks that I had only dreamed of on earth! And Simcha...oh my goodness. Let's just say the angel could *shred!* I've never had so much fun in my life. Nathan is going to love this.

Eventually we decided to go back to my home. As we slalomed down the mountain, I had such control over the board, I could easily talk to Simcha as I maneuvered.

"That was just *awesome!*" I grinned at him, and carved around a tree. He carved around the other side and swooped back next to me.

"I've been waiting to snowboard with you since you arrived." He laughed.

"Wow! Everything was so perfect. The runs, the pipe, the powder. You sure know how to have fun for an angel."

He dodged around a little rabbit dashing out from behind a tree and then gave me a gentlemanly bow (still cruising down the hillside.) I laughed again.

"It's so wild. I always thought my honeymoon would be something like this," I said, voicing my thoughts.

He just smiled a knowing smile.

"I always wanted to go to a ski resort somewhere exclusive like Vale or Aspen and have one of those crazy honeymoons where you just snowboard and have fun the whole time."

"Danielle, when we get back, the Lord has requested your private company, if it suits you?" Simcha asked gently.

"Y-yeah, of course." I smiled. I wondered what Jesus wanted to meet about.

In a minute we sprayed snow all over the back deck as we slid to a stop, laughing all the way. Simcha unstrapped his bindings and escorted me up to the house. He took me to the living room, where he gave another slight bow, and then retreated. Jesus was standing in the middle of the room as I walked in. He motioned playfully with His head for me to join Him. He had such a wonderful way of always making me feel at home.

As I walked up, He said, "Can I show you something special?" Jesus seemed really excited.

"Of course." I smiled, full of anticipation. The passion in His eyes told me this was something really close to His heart. He took my hand, and just like with the vision Simcha showed me, a sort of shimmering screen opened before us. This time I saw the most gorgeous wedding dress I had ever laid eyes on.

The lines undulated in and out of a design that was the pure expression of a Master Craftsman. The fabric flowed from layers of silk, to lace, to a material that could only be described as heavenly. It glistened and shimmered all the colors of the rainbow—and more. There were colors I had never seen before...the most beautiful, vibrant colors. Then I realized juxtaposing this gleaming fabric were sparkling jewels sewn right into the dress. Rubies and emeralds and jasper and topaz and diamonds...*so* many diamonds. They glowed with a brilliance and pride of being included in what was clearly a royal wedding gown. Off to the side was the most beautiful diadem. It's difficult to explain heavenly beauty, but this made any Disney princess's crown seem like dollar store junk. The very gold it was fashioned from was pulsing in patterns that represented different aspects of

Heaven's royalty. God's throne was visible on one side and on the other was the most delicate dove—the Holy Spirit!

I looked over at Jesus and He was lost in a smile so saturated in love. I flinched and His eyes came back to the moment. The shimmering vision-screen dissipated.

"Whoa," was all I could manage.

"My bride is so beautiful," He said, with a tender look in His eyes.

"That dress is for your bride?" I was still amazed.

"Oh yes. It's not finished yet. It's going to be even more exquisite. My bride is growing even more exquisite. "

I knew enough scripture to know He was talking about His church. I remembered reading about the magnificent marriage imagery in the Bible. The great marriage feast of the Lamb and His bride is to be the crescendo of creation. It is God's way of celebrating when the Lord's work is complete, and we have joined Him in our eternal home. The imagery showed Jesus as a groom and His church as a bride. I wondered for a second at how the entire church, from times ancient to the time whenever the Lord returns for His people still on earth, would be like a bride. It was something I couldn't really wrap my mind around, but I resolved to understanding this mystery soon. Perhaps Simcha could help me.

He turned to me and He looked directly into my eyes.

"Danielle, I know you wanted to get married."

I froze at these words. It was the one thing I would really have liked to experience on earth. I did indeed want to be a wife to a wonderful man. I wanted to have a beautiful wedding and have Ashley as my maid of honor.

"Lord Jesus, I'm not sad, but the experience of being a bride would have been so wonderful."

He stepped back and took my face in both of His hands and gazed into my eyes. "You will my love. You will."

"What...how, Lord? What do You mean?" I was almost beside myself by now.

"Danielle, that dress is for *you*." A wave of heat washed over me and I gasped.

"Lord, what do You mean?" I repeated. My head was swimming.

"Danielle, the dress and the diadem is for you!" I was entirely overwhelmed by a love that seemed to emanate straight from His heart and simply enraptured me. I thought I was going to fall at His feet and my knees buckled. Jesus stepped in and caught me and drew me into His embrace.

"It's for you Danielle. You are my Church. Every believer is my Church. You are my bride."

I sank into His arms and reeled from the waves of love and glory washing over my soul. I felt so holy, so individually treasured, and so royal.

Eventually He put me down and there was simply nothing else to do but bow my knees before Him. In an instant, I glimpsed His Kingship and it rippled through my very core. He was so majestic, so regal—yet so gentle and humble. It was tangible to me now. Jesus had long ago proven Himself to be the most humble of all servants and that is why God established Him as the most mighty ruler of every living being.

Chapter Eleven:

FAITH IN GOD'S SOVEREIGNTY

———∞∞∞———

E ight months after the accident, I wrote the following paragraph on Danielle's website:

> An area where God has been working in me is my
> own faith. Praising God through the tough times,
> trusting in His sovereignty, and experiencing peace
> in the midst of tragedy is only possible through faith.
> God didn't cause the accident, but He allowed it.
> And...He didn't make a mistake by allowing Danielle
> to die. The accident does not change the greatness
> of God. His ways are always right, even when they
> don't make sense from my perspective. Danielle's
> death has strengthened my faith and helped me to
> trust and depend on God at a new level.

My grief journey was not complete until I was able to have
unflinching faith in God's sovereignty and omniscience. When
I was able to trust in God's divine sovereignty, I could rest in
the truth that everything is under God's control and nothing
happens without His direction or permission. I believe this
truth is wonderfully illustrated by King David in Psalm 103:19:
"The Lord has established His throne in the heavens, and His
sovereignty rules over all." NASB

God is good and He only does what is absolutely just and right. These words come easily when life is going smoothly, but when you are awakened by a police officer to inform you that your daughter has died in a car accident, or you are told by your physician that you have cancer, or you were sexually abused—those words become more difficult to say. For as long as I have had children, I have prayed daily for protection over them. My initial reaction was, "Why didn't You intervene, God? You could have saved her."

I know God can do nothing wrong and that, according to Matthew 19:26, "with God, all things are possible." He is omnipotent (all-powerful.) He could have intervened in Danielle's accident and she would be here with me today. The fact, however, that God is all-powerful does not mean that we are robots and He dictates everything. He certainly didn't want Danielle to drink and drive, and Danielle made her own poor choice that led to the accident. What God permits may not be His best plan, but I am confident that when He does permit a tragedy that seemingly doesn't make sense, He will accomplish good out of the evil. Many of us are grieving losses that are due to sinful actions and the pervasive evil we encounter every day.

Joni Eareckson Tada's statement helped me envision the behind the scenes redemptive work that God is orchestrating in Danielle's story and many of your stories. "His plans are being accomplished despite, yes, even through, these trag-edies. ...He loathes the wickedness and misery and destruc-tion itself—but he has determined to steer what he hates to accomplish what he loves."[16]

God's sovereignty became a real comfort to me, knowing that nothing touches us that His watchful eye doesn't see. We can surrender our troubles back to His control, knowing our lives are under the authority of a loving, eternal God.

A situation most parents will understand helped deepen my grasp on the concept. Danielle had jaundice, a common condition in newborns, and the doctor had to draw blood from the heel of her foot when she was only three days old.

I held her as the doctor pierced her heel. Danielle went from calm and trusting to screaming hysterically and looking at me with terrified eyes that begged, *How can you let this happen to me*? I was in tears knowing how much she was hurting, and while I was tempted to stop the doctor, I knew it was for Danielle's benefit that she go through this (even though she couldn't understand what was going on). As I held my crying child, I felt such intense love and concern for her. But I knew within a few moments the pain would be over.

When I think back to those nights I spent crying, over-whelmed with grief over the loss of Danielle, I can imagine my Lord Jesus was weeping with me, feeling such intense love for His child, but also knowing this pain would soon be over. Of course, "soon" is a relative term, and I use it in comparison to an eternity with no tears and no sorrow. I allowed the physician to draw Danielle's blood, fully aware that my precious baby would be in pain. Just like Danielle didn't understand why she was hurting, many of us don't understand why we suffer.

God may not step in and intervene to change the effects of sin that affect people, seemingly at random. It is beyond us to grasp every intricacy of God's ways of justice and love. The hope of believers is that we draw on God's promises to get us through these tough times.

I have heard from many confused people who know they serve a powerful God, and yet He doesn't heal a loved one they have been praying for. Satan loves to take advantage of these situations to whisper, "God does not care." This is *not* truth.

Randy Alcorn reminds us that our faith should not be focused on the result we're so desperately seeking; it should be trusting in God's infinite wisdom.

> Insisting on knowing the unknowable dooms us to frustration and resentment toward God. ...We lack God's omniscience, omnipotence, wisdom, holiness, justice, and goodness. If we insist we have the right, or even assume we have the capacity to

understand the hidden purposes of God, we forfeit the comfort and perspective we could have had in kneeling before his vastly superior wisdom. ...God's answer is beyond our understanding.[17]

The Bible has many verses that show we do not have the capacity to grasp God's infinite mind, nor question His ways. This one is among my favorites: "'For my thoughts are not your thoughts, neither are your ways my ways,' declares the LORD. 'As the heavens are higher than the earth, so are my ways higher than your ways and my thoughts than your thoughts'" *(*Isaiah 55:8-9).

My friend Gayle, whom I mentioned earlier, went home to be with the Lord after battling cancer for many years. During the years of her struggle, she kept a journal, in which she wrote her thoughts on faith:

> I've been meditating on Hebrews 11 these past couple of weeks. I think the first verse clearly states exactly how I feel, "Now faith is confidence in what we hope for and assurance about what we do not see." I feel VERY certain that the God of the Universe has the power to heal all our diseases since all things are under His loving, grace-filled dominion. Chapter 11 also reveals that He can shut the mouths of lions, water molecules stood on end to form two walls of water so that a million people could cross the Red Sea, walls tumbled down at His comman, mothers received their children back from the dead, all through FAITH in God Almighty. So there is no doubt in my mind that God can bestow His Healing Hand and I could wake up healed someday. However, the closing verses of Hebrews 11 in verses 39 and 40 puts it all into a balanced perspective stating that although they were approved by God through faith they did not receive the promises of God before they died, for

God had something better. And knowing what an incredible, incorruptible, wise, and grace-filled God that we have, His 'better' can be trusted even if it means that physical healing here on earth does not occur.

I'm reminded of Abraham, the father of faith. Abraham was talking to God one evening and the Lord said, (paraphrased) "Abraham, someday your descendants will be more numerous than the stars you see in the sky." That must have been confusing. He didn't have any children and was getting old rapidly. Then God became silent as the years went by. Finally Isaac, the miracle son was born. It didn't end there, though. In Genesis 22, Abraham was having another chat with God and was told by God to sacrifice Isaac. Can you imagine the questions he had? There is no record of God saying, "I know this sounds confusing, but trust me, there will be a happy ending." No, Abraham had to struggle with this all by himself. It didn't make sense, but he continued to believe and have faith.

Abraham didn't completely understand all the ways of God, but he did know that God would do right. God showed Abraham the future didn't depend on Isaac. It depended on God. My future doesn't depend on my family or whether my dreams come true. My future depends on God.

It encourages and inspires me so much to read about people in the Bible who trusted God regardless of the outcome. Shadrach, Meshack and Abednego were devout Israelites who refused to bow down to an idol even though they knew this would cost them their lives. Their response in Daniel 3:16-18 is a response I wish I could always have: "Shadrach, Meshach and Abednego replied to him, 'King Nebuchadnezzar, we do not need to defend ourselves before you in this matter. If we are thrown into the blazing furnace, the God we serve is able to deliver us from it, and he will deliver us from Your Majesty's hand. *But even if he does not,* we want you to know, Your Majesty, that we will not serve your gods or worship the image of gold you have set up.'" (emphasis mine)

I certainly do pray for God to supernaturally intervene. But when I pray for something, I ask God to help me be willing to accept His answer. I have come to understand that there will be a time in each of our lives (for most of us, multiple times) when we will face a crisis of faith. At those times, our beliefs about God will collide with a painful situation. We may question the goodness of God or whether we can trust Him. What is happening does not make sense from our point of view. I personally have to cling tenaciously to the conviction that God is good, and make the decision to completely trust God, even when I don't understand.

Beth Moore, in her book *Daniel: Lives of Integrity, Words Of Prophecy*[18] talked about how fiery trials can refine our faith, whether we're delivered *from* the fire, delivered *through* the fire, or delivered *by* the fire into His arms. Satan wanted to destroy my faith; however, God has used the accident to refine my faith.

Many of you may be desperate for a word of hope. I can assure you that God is to be trusted, and He loves and cares for you more deeply than you can fathom. In my pain and confusion about why God didn't intervene in the accident, I had to choose to trust Him. As a result, He has carried me through the darkest valley I have ever experienced.

Chapter Twelve:

OUR RESPONSE TO LOSS

—∞∞∞—

No one is immune to pain and trials, and most of us at some point will face a devastating loss. I'm referring to more than a loss of a loved one. Loss includes illness, disability, divorce, abuse, unemployment, and a rebellious child. Whatever form it takes, a difficult loss is painful.

Most people don't have a choice in the loss, but we do have a choice in how we respond to the loss. How we respond to loss and what we let it do to us has the potential to either destroy us or transform us. We can allow anger, resentment, and hopelessness to control our lives, or we can allow the Holy Spirit to be our comforter as we grieve and experience healing and renewal.

The importance of our thoughts cannot be stressed enough. Our moods, feelings, and actions are influenced by our thoughts. Very quickly, we can fall into a vicious cycle of exponentially negative thoughts if we don't exercise control over what we think about. I couldn't change the reality of Danielle's death, but I could influence my thinking. The Bible speaks to the significance of our thoughts in Romans 12:2: "Do not conform to the pattern of this world, but be transformed by the renewing of your mind. Then you will be able to test and approve what God's will is—his good, pleasing and perfect will."

Daniel Amen in his book, *Change Your Brain Change Your Life*, talks about how our mind has a certain tone based on the types of thoughts we think:

> People who are depressed have one dispiriting thought following another. When they look at the past, they feel regret. When they look at the future, they feel anxiety and pessimism. In the present moment, they're bound to find something unsatisfactory. The lens through which they see themselves, others, and the world has a dim grayness to it. They are suffering from automatic negative thoughts.[19]

We all engage in self-talk or automatic thoughts. These are the words that we use to describe and interpret our world. Most people are not aware of their self-talk unless they make a concerted effort to tune into it. If our self-talk is negative, and we continue to allow ourselves to brood, we will stay stuck in a morass of painful and self-defeating thought patterns.

A strategy to enhance positive thoughts is called "thought stopping." This involves catching yourself in the midst of the negative thoughts and saying (or thinking) "Stop!" This interrupts the pattern of negativity and allows you to distract yourself with another activity or positive thought. It may help to write on a card verses such as Philippians 4:6-8 and pull out this card whenever you start to think negative thoughts.

> Do not be anxious about anything, but in every situation, by prayer and petition, with thanksgiving, present your requests to God. And the peace of God, which transcends all understanding, will guard your hearts and your minds in Christ Jesus. Finally, brothers and sisters, whatever is true, whatever is noble, whatever is right, whatever is pure, whatever is lovely, whatever is admirable—if anything is excellent or praiseworthy—think about such things.

Negative thoughts creating emotional distress almost always contain distortions, although they appear valid to the thinker. It often helps to seek advice from a counselor or pastor if you are struggling with your thought patterns. They can help you to recognize negative or dysfunctional thoughts and substitute new ways of thinking and responding.

I'll share one thought that could have continued to consume me and pull me down. Because Danielle's death occurred without warning, I initially struggled with a paralyzing fear that the trauma could repeat itself. Ashley and Nathan's safety was constantly on my mind. To prevent such a fear from taking root in my thought process, I reminded myself of verses such as Psalm 112:7: "They will have no fear of bad news; their hearts are steadfast, trusting in the LORD."

Other thoughts that can block progress toward healing are when we continue to relive and rehearse the past. We can liken this to driving our car forward by looking in the rear view mirror.

We cannot change the past, and we don't have to carry the past into the future. God talks about this in Isaiah 43:18-19: "Forget about what's happened; don't keep going over old history. Be alert, be present. I'm about to do something brand-new. It's bursting out! Don't you see it? There it is! I'm making a road through the desert, rivers in the badlands." (MSG)

We may feel we have the right to remain bitter, vengeful, and full of blame, but these destructive thoughts and emotions only hurt us. Compounded effects of focusing persistently on negative thoughts can result in prolonged depression.

Another dangerous emotion is self-pity. Continuing in a pattern of wanting everyone to feel sorry for you can be addictive. When Jesus is given control of your life, His love and mercy will pierce your wounded soul and allow you to release a torrent of bitterness and self-pity that has festered there. Joni Erickson Tada described a time of deep despair after the first year of lying paralyzed in the hospital. She recalls the moment when she called out to God, "God, if I can't die, please show me how to live."[20] That was the beginning of her emotional healing. The self-pity and anger she had felt turned into feelings of hope. God wants us to cry out to Him. He hears our pleas.

Managing my thoughts was a struggle, though. As anyone who has experienced loss can relate, at times it seemed like my moods were on steroids. One evening when I was struggling with incredible irritability, I grabbed a book that had been very influential in my life years ago, called *Lord Change Me,* by Evelyn Christianson. She compares our emotions and behaviors to thermometers and thermostats:

> So much of the time we are like thermometers, registering the temperature of the atmosphere around us. We respond to a cold shoulder, a chilly remark, a cool reception with a plunge of our own thermometers. Or a hot accusation influences us to flash back with a hotter retaliation...But when we let God change us into what He wants us to be, we become thermostats—changing the climate around us, not just registering it. And when it is God who sets the dial, our environment always changes for the better....a cold piercing glance turns into a tender look, a sharp tongue utters a soft answer.[21]

This illustration reinforced the truth that we can choose joy and kindness. Even though we may feel justified in being irritable, we can show love in the middle of the toughest time of our life. When I think of individuals who I greatly admire, I find that their attitude is what sets them apart. They were able to rise above the circumstances. Heartaches and setbacks did not deter them from leaving the past behind and choosing joy.

Charles Swindoll's writing on attitude describes this truth well:

> The longer I live, the more I realize the importance of choosing the right attitude in life. Attitude is more important than facts. It is more important than

your past; more important than your education or your financial situation; more important than your circumstances, your successes, or your failures; more important than what other people think or say or do. It is more important than your appearance, your giftedness, or your skills. It will make or break a company. It will cause a church to soar or sink. It will make the difference between a happy home or a miserable home. You have a choice each day regarding the attitude you will embrace.

Life is like a violin. You can focus on the broken strings that dangle, or you can play your life's melody on the one that remains. You cannot change the years that have passed, nor can you change the daily tick of the clock. You cannot change the pace of your march toward your death. You cannot change the decisions or reactions of other people. And you certainly cannot change the inevitable. Those are strings that dangle! What you <u>can</u> do is play on the one string that remains—your attitude. I am convinced that life is 10 percent what happens to me and 90 percent how I react to it. The same is true for you.[22]

"Danielle, can you tell how deeply I love you?" As Jesus spoke, adoration completely overwhelmed my heart.

"I'm not sure I fully comprehend it completely, my Lord, but yes, it's deeper than I ever imagined."

He took my hand and we walked over and sat on my beautiful couch. I pulled my knees up to my chest and wrapped my arms around them. Jesus sat sideways on the couch and faced me.

"Why do you think it's easier for you to grasp My love now?" He asked.

I had to think about it for a second. The obvious answer was because I was in His presence. In Heaven, His love fills the atmosphere. But I knew there was something deeper or He wouldn't be asking me so pointedly.

"Is it because we have no distractions here, Lord?"

He smiled proudly and nodded. "Yes, my precious child. On earth, many enemies of mine, and therefore yours, are present. They work to sow bitterness, strife, jealousy, hatred, and all forms of evil."

I didn't want to think about any of that, but I knew there was a lesson here.

"The enemy wants to stifle people with lies so their thoughts become a mess that controls them. But the good news is people can gain control over their thoughts by believing the truths in My Word and relying on the power of the Holy Spirit to help them." There was a joy in the way He said this, but somehow coupled with an urgency.

I sat thinking about this for a few seconds. In my life, I often knew when I struggled the most with troubling thoughts was usually when I wasn't spending time reading the Bible and praying.

"Is that why everything is so wonderful here, Lord... because there is only good and no one struggles with negative thoughts?"

He smiled and nodded. "Yes. It's one of the reasons. Nothing unclean can enter those gates."

I had been living in the atmosphere of indescribable peace and pure euphoric joy for a while now, but when I considered it would be for eternity, my mind reeled. The joy grew exponentially.

Jesus saw my expression and laughed loudly. His laugh was so wonderful; you couldn't help but laugh with Him. We started laughing and laughing, almost unable to stop.

"Lord..." I gasped. "We're going to live like this forever!" It seemed wonderfully hilarious for some reason. The joy continued to rise and made me swoon. I laughed even harder at this.

"I couldn't be depressed if I tried!" I screeched out loud. Jesus guffawed again and buried His face in my shoulder. My body was shaking I was laughing so hard. I looked out my back window at the snowcapped mountains. I wanted to send my family a postcard, but I knew a postcard couldn't come close to capturing this. Suddenly, the deepest peace descended on me like a warm, cozy blanket and I sank back in the chair, still gazing out the window.

I was smiling when I turned to Him. "Lord, I wish I knew this peace, joy, and love when I lived on earth." I began. "That sad old planet would be changed in a week if people experienced this."

"People can experience true joy and peace, right there on earth, Danielle."

"I wish they would," I whispered. I knew how tough it was living in the middle of a fallen world. Sooner or later, the worries rub off on you, and you end up trying to medicate them with cheap worldly alternatives that lead to sin. *If they could just grasp this love and peace,* I thought.

"They can have this peace, Danielle." Jesus said softly.

I looked at Him, realizing I still didn't really know how.

"My Word is alive. It is My heart in written form. The more My Word gets into someone, the deeper My Spirit can work in them. They can experience peace. They just have to meditate on My Word—think My thoughts—and spend time talking to Me."

I exhaled deeply, thinking about the opportunities that were available to those on earth. The Bible talks about being transformed by the renewing of our minds. If only they recognized the importance of filling their minds with godly thoughts.

"You are growing so well, My child," Jesus said to me. I wanted to learn so much more about Him and the mysteries of God. I was about to ask Him another question when He stood up and said, "I've got a great surprise for you. Come, let's go!"

I was just beginning to want to stretch my legs a bit, so I nodded eagerly. "What is it, Lord?" I asked jumping up and off the couch.

"Danielle..." Jesus made a (playful) wearied face. "When are you going to learn a surprise is a secret!"

I laughed again and we headed out the front door.

———∞∞———

I'd like to make you a little more aware of the role that Satan's sinister forces can play in our thoughts. It should come as no surprise that the enemy has made our minds the bull's-eye of his target. His primary weapon is to try to strangle us with deceit and negatively influence our thoughts. We often believe these lies more when we are wounded. And as I'm sure many of us are aware, we're capable of having an extremely dark thought life without the light of Christ illuminating our minds. On May 17th, 2008, Satan not only wanted to destroy Danielle but also our family. He wanted to steal our joy and see us feeling hopeless so that we would give up on our faith. I know the importance of vigilantly guarding my mind against negative thoughts, and I pray against these attacks daily.

Another important aspect of our response to loss relates to individual beliefs and assumptions, which give us a standard against which to frame our life experiences. Often, these assumptions are severely challenged after a loss. One of my assumptions, which many parents have, was that my children would die after me. When our assumptions are shattered, we may begin to feel vulnerable and begin to question many aspects of life, including our faith.

Another false assumption is the belief that if I follow Christ and His teachings, no tragedy will happen to me. God tells us in the Bible that we will endure trials in this lifetime; yet He promises us that His grace is sufficient to carry us through whatever we face. If we have built our life on inaccurate assumptions, we have been set up for disillusionment. Facing a loss is often a time where we re-evaluate what we once thought was true. It is the perfect opportunity to create a new foundation based on God's truth.

The Search For Meaning

> Our shattered dreams are never random. They are always a piece in a larger puzzle, a chapter in a larger story. Pain is a tragedy. But it's never only a tragedy. For the Christian, it's always a necessary mile on the long journey to joy. …A new way to live is available to us, a way that leads to a joy-filled encounter with Christ, to a life-arousing community with others, and to a powerful transformation of our interior worlds that makes us more like Jesus.[23]

Many counselors feel the process of working through the pain of grief is not complete until the grieving person has found meaning in their grief. This includes obtaining an understanding of the loss, reappraising your identity, and discovering renewed purpose. When we experience a devastating loss, we often struggle with a severe crisis of meaning, and we search for how to reinvest in life when our prior goals and purposes have been challenged.

Unfortunately, many tragedies appear senseless and meaningless, and as a result, many of our foundational beliefs collapse under the pain we are experiencing. There will be many of you who will say, "I don't see any good coming from my tragedy." When there doesn't appear to be any purpose to the pain, it is significantly more difficult to endure. The factor that strips a person's faith isn't necessarily the pain, but it's often the lack of meaning and purpose that makes the situation so unbearable. Martyrs and military heroes have endured significant suffering, including sacrificing their lives, because they believed the suffering will count for something. Jim Elliot, who was speared to death by the Auca people in Ecuador, described the ultimate, eternal investment that turns martyrdom into a victory. "He is no fool who gives what he cannot keep to gain what he cannot lose." He clearly saw the eternal purpose of suffering.

So how do we find meaning in suffering and begin to see the ultimate, eternal investment of suffering well? Joseph's story was helpful as I reflected on all the suffering he experienced, and yet he could say to his brothers in Genesis 50:20: "You intended to harm me, but God intended it for good to accomplish what is now being done, the saving of many lives." God had a purpose and could use even their evil intentions to fulfill His Kingdom purpose. I am certain, however, that when Joseph was sold into slavery by his own brothers, was wrongly accused by an adulteress, and sat in jail for years that he may have struggled to see the meaning of these events.

Similarly, God would use the horrific pain I experienced. The accident disrupted my version of my story, including hopes and dreams that included Danielle. My safe bubble of assumptions had been burst. Finding new meaning and purpose required adjusting my dreams. My life certainly has not unfolded in the way I was hoping it would. However, God has given me a different opportunity, a different territory. It wasn't easy to reinvest myself in a world without Danielle, and finding renewed purpose absolutely does not erase the sadness that I still often feel.

Finding meaning in a loss or trial doesn't necessarily mean that you start up a ministry. God can use you in so many different ways. I was reminded of this truth when reading a story by Joni Erickson Tada. She described a conversation with her friend Karla, who had both legs amputated, a kidney transplant, collapsed veins, and is legally blind. Karla was questioning her use on this earth and was wondering why God hasn't taken her home. Joni responded by reminding her that God has His reasons, and used Philippians 1:22-24: "If I am to go on living in the body, this will mean fruitful labor for me. Yet what shall I choose? I do not know! I am torn between the two: I desire to depart and be with Christ, which is better by far; but it is more necessary for you that I remain in the body." Joni explained to Karla that it is necessary to remain here because others benefit and learn from her things of eternal importance. "When we suffer and handle it with grace, we're like walking billboards advertising the positive way God works in the life of someone who suffers."[24]

There may be some of you who are ready to go to your heavenly home and not sure how much longer you can bear the trials you are facing. Take comfort in knowing that even when your personal world seems to be a mess, you may be ministering to others who are noticing your perseverance through pain. As you press on imperfectly, but faithfully seeking Jesus through your trials, you are giving others a window into the love and power of God.

Chapter Thirteen:

CONNECTING TO SOURCES OF COMFORT

---∞∞∞---

The power of support

I was blessed to have truly wonderful family and friends who were there for us when we desperately needed help. They cried with me, delivered countless meals, and kept in contact through phone calls, emails, and cards. I'll never forget the day some friends held a special luncheon, showered me with pink gifts, and had a very special time of prayer and blessing.

Another creative example of love was a friend who was aware that one of Danielle's gifts was to encourage others. She hosted an "encouragement" party where we shared Danielle stories, and then had an opportunity to write encouragement cards to others. I can't express enough how these personal touches impacted my healing.

Even Jesus desperately needed the comfort of His closest friends the night He was betrayed. Matthew 26:37 shows us this: "He took Peter and the two sons of Zebedee along with him, and he began to be sorrowful and troubled. Then he said to them, 'My soul is overwhelmed with sorrow to the point of death. Stay here and keep watch with me.'" Unfortunately, His disciples were unable to stay awake and support Him during this incredible time of grief. I read this passage after going through the loss of Danielle, and thanked God for the true friends I have who "stayed awake" with me during the deep, dark valley that I faced.

Having caring people in your life who will give you their time is important. Please don't underestimate the significance of your support system. But some of the responsibility rests on you. I feel one of the reasons I had such an ongoing out-pouring of love and support is that I sent out periodic emails to friends, sharing how I was doing and letting them know how they could specifically pray for the family. I also shared what was helpful for me. For example, I let others know that it was healing for me to hear them talk about Danielle. Keeping her memory alive is important, and I cherished the memories others had. It may be difficult, but it's important for us to com-municate our needs to others. Sometimes we need to show those who care about us *how* to care for us. It is helpful to write down your physical, emotional, and spiritual needs, and then communicate these needs to others.

I have been overwhelmed by those who have been with me for the long haul—those who continue to support me, years later, particularly on special dates. That, however, is typically not the experience of most people. Most receive the bulk of their support for a few weeks and then the calls and cards stop. From my experience as a counselor and throughout my own journey with loss, I have seen how this can create a sense of isolation which can quickly become unhealthy for someone grieving. If we have very few people in our lives to support us at a time of loss, it may be necessary to consider joining a grief group, which can be a safe place to share feelings. Even with all of the ongoing support I have had, I found a grief group tremendously beneficial.

People don't always do or say helpful things—even when their intent is to be caring. On a few occasions, I have had to remember and accept that no one is perfect. I cannot expect others to appreciate how sensitive I am or how raw my emotions may be at any given moment. Most people make comments because they care about us. We can choose to give grace and receive these comments as gifts of love, even those that may not have been helpful.

There have also been times when I wanted to withdraw from others and build a protective wall around myself. Like for all those who are grieving, it is important for me to be honest with my feelings and respond to my need for processing my sorrow in solitude sometimes. This is a very natural reaction. However, pulling away too often or for too long is not healthy for anyone and leaves hearts and minds vulnerable. God has shown me over and over again how important it is for grieving people to share their stories with others. That is how comfort and encouragement are exchanged while empathy and insight grow.

Journaling

As I've mentioned, journaling was helpful in my healing. It allowed me to express my feelings, my heart's desires and prayers and also gave me a place to list sources of comfort. During that first year after Danielle's death, I journaled almost 200 pages. I didn't go back to read my journal until over a year later. I vividly remember the day I read it. I made a cup of my favorite tea, settled down in a comfy chair and began reading. With tears flooding my eyes, I was amazed at the common thread woven throughout this bittersweet tapestry. I saw how God was with me every step of the way.

Later, I read a book by Mary Beth Chapman. She and her husband, singer-songwriter Steven Curtis Chapman, faced the loss of their daughter, Maria, in a tragic car accident just four days after Danielle's accident. In her book, she expressed exactly how I felt while reading my journal, and seeing God's presence throughout my grief journey.

> God really is with us and for us. I have found that even during those times when the path is darkest, He leaves little bits of evidence along the way— bread crumbs of grace—that can give me what I need to take the next step.[25]

Writing down memories of your loved one is a special process that can help with healing. Initially, the memories may be vivid, but over time they fade. Writing them down ensures that you never lose them. A few months after Danielle's death, Nathan came to me with sad eyes and said, "I don't ever want to forget Danielle." I encouraged him to write down his memories of Danielle. The first memory that he mentioned was snowboarding with her. He said, "I remember when we raced each other down the hill." I chuckled, remembering that Danielle had quite the competitive streak in her.

As Nathan and I talked about racing down the hill, 2 Timothy 4:7 came to mind: "I have fought the good fight, I have finished the race, I have kept the faith." This is the verse we used for Danielle's tombstone inscription. Paul was talking about the race of life and I had assumed I would finish this race before my children. Sadly, Danielle finished before me, a reminder that the duration of our life's race is uncertain, but we do have control over how well we run.

In my journal I included the emails I received from Danielle's friends, sharing memories and making reference to the impact Danielle had on their lives. I'd like to share one letter written to Danielle by a friend. It was given to me two days after the accident, at a moment where I was feeling incredible grief and desperately needed to be lifted up by God. Here is one paragraph:

> One of the memories that I will hold closest to my heart was last June, almost one year ago. I was making a lot of bad decisions in my life including [personal details omitted]. I trusted you and had confided in you about everything that was going on in my life. You told me about some of the mistakes you had made in your own life, and how God had recaptured your heart over the past year and had helped you to realize that He had bigger plans for you. You had always had an evident love for Jesus, but that day at Starbucks you talked about Him with

such conviction. God was doing amazing work in you! You were there to listen, encourage, and pray for me.

I read this letter and wept, thanking God for allowing me to continue to see additional glimpses into Danielle's life.

Reaching out to others

As our emotional pain begins to lessen, we can help to heal our own grief by reaching out to others who are hurting. If we have experienced a loss, we are uniquely qualified to show compassion to others. One of the greatest gifts we can give to someone is to listen.

Making myself available to others has been a significant contributor to my healing. A friend called three weeks after the accident and told me about a mom who had also just lost a child. My heart broke for that mom and I called her. As I listened to her pain and tried to encourage her, my focus moved from my pain to hers. It was then I realized a wonderful side effect of investing in others is that it will also give you a renewed sense of purpose.

There were many sources of comfort for me, but I will close this chapter by saying God is clearly the best comforter. In John 14:16, Jesus says He'll send us a Comforter, the Holy Spirit. We can cling to this truth as we travel the journey of grief. God is faithful to heal and restore us. We will go through many trials as believers, but one thing is certain: God will never leave us nor forsake us.

———ꙮ———

Jesus was so excited, He half-dragged me out of the house and up the road, back toward the city center.

"Lord! What can possibly be so exciting?" I laughed. I knew by now that there were a million possibilities in this wonderful place.

"I want you to meet someone," He said.

"Oooh. Who is it Jesus?" I expected Him to tease me again about not waiting for surprises.

"Someone you really admire," He said, as He tugged at my hand again.

In no time we were back on the golden streets and heading towards what I could sense was the very center of the city. All around us were beautiful houses, with the most exquisite and unique gardens I'd ever seen. A little band of children formed behind us and Jesus spoke lovingly to them. He even scooped up a few, hugging them while we walked. As we passed various people, they either bowed down in pure adoration and reverence or waved happily at our Lord. Some wore modern clothing, some wore beautiful, but peculiar clothing I couldn't place. Others wore long robes. It is just something you perceive, but He knew every one of these people personally and loved them deeply. Behind each wave and each smile was a deep connection, like the one I had with Him. Eventually the street brought us to the most beautiful sight.

In a huge square were literally thousands of people. At the center was a huge series of built up steps in stunning, intricate, geometric designs. Hundreds of people were sitting on them, or gathered eagerly around others who seemed to be teaching and discussing. Groups of musicians and singers played their instruments and sang, all clearly worshiping the Lord with their art. The most astonishing part was that, even though I could tell there were several keys being played, they were all in complete harmony. The sense of community was so enthralling, I just stood there for several seconds, taking it all in.

Of course, as soon as Jesus made an appearance, everyone roared with joy and their song became one huge melody of praise. I suddenly realized I was again joining in, knowing intuitively the most exquisite tune. I could tell, however, that everyone sensed Jesus was there for a specific purpose and didn't throng about Him as the children were inclined to do. But it was impossible for them not to adore and worship Him as we made our way to the steps. I felt the strongest love emanating out of Him, sort of in waves, as He smiled individually and lovingly at everyone we passed.

We kept climbing around what were clearly groups of teachers and students. As we stepped up and around people, my heart began to flutter. I recognized some of these teachers simply by their *presence* as we walked by. One was, without a doubt, the prophet Jeremiah. I had read his book and could somehow just tell that it was Jeremiah teaching a group of men and women. He looked so full of joy. He even smiled and nodded to me. There was no one like Jesus but I felt an exciting sense of being a little star-struck. These were the *heroes* of our faith and they were more real than ever! We passed the most striking woman intently explaining something to another group. As I stared at her, I realized this was Queen Esther! She also paused and bowed her head gracefully to Jesus and then smiled at me. After passing several others, I saw we had finally come to the top of the step structure.

I saw a fairly stocky man with a longer beard than most, sitting in the center of a large group. I could immediately tell he commanded a great amount of authority, and had been teaching for a long time. At the same time, he seemed to be entirely humble and acting in service to those sitting around him. As we neared him, he paused and looked up at our Lord. In the man's eyes was the deepest, purest love I had yet seen for the Lord. It was as if everything around him had disappeared and he existed only for the whim of His Master. I tore my gaze away from him and looked up at Jesus. The Lord's eyes were locked onto his and a broad smile had spread across His face. I sensed this man knew Jesus deeply and had a very unique relationship with Him. I felt a compulsion to know Jesus like this man knew Him.

"My King," he said, as we walked up. He spoke for the group, who all assumed postures of reverence and complete love.

"My faithful brother." Jesus smiled. "Still working hard as ever for the Kingdom, I see?"

"Your work is truly the only pleasure I need to know, my Lord." He smiled. Jesus grinned widely again. These two had clearly been through some stuff together.

"Do you have time to share some truth of your experience with Danielle?" Jesus asked.

"It would be my privilege, Lord," the man said, and looked over at me curiously.

"She has some knotty questions, whose answers I believe you are uniquely qualified to help her untie."

I do? I thought. The man looked at me thoughtfully and nodded.

"Yes, my Lord. Whatever You need."

Jesus nodded gratefully. It was a subtle thing, I noticed, but He could have simply *told* the man to help me, and he would have jumped. Instead He asked him. Jesus was the perfect gentleman.

"Danielle." The Lord turned to me. "This is James. He is a faithful servant of mine and my Kingdom and wrote a very influential letter to My church."

"Yes, Lord," I said quickly. I wanted to say "I know," but I think everyone knew I perceived it was James.

"He can help you understand the deeper mysteries of my kingdom. His schedule is quite full, so this is a valuable opportunity."

I had never thought about what we're going to do in Heaven, but one thing that was clear was we were going to keep learning about Jesus and the mysteries of God's kingdom. This was a "duh" moment for me, but I had really never thought about it.

As I was pondering all of this, I realized James and his companions were looking up, smiling at me. Jesus said, "I'll be back for you in a bit, My child. Enjoy yourself." With that He squeezed my hand and walked back down the steps.

"So you have some questions?" James asked, invitingly.

"Well, I...I'm not sure I'd call them *deep*," I stuttered. I wasn't overwhelmed, but this was JAMES! He was like a Bible rock star! He motioned to the step next to him, and moved over a little.

"Please, my dear, sit down."

I sat next to him and grinned sheepishly at those around us. They all seemed to be very intrigued with what Jesus Himself had brought me over to ask. I had no idea what to say, but didn't feel nervous.

"You just graduated?" James asked, breaking the ice.

"Huh? Oh no...I had just taken some finals when..." I thought this was a strange question to ask. Then I realized what he was talking about. "OH! Yes, haha..." I giggled feeling a little silly, but they all laughed with me. "*Graduated*...yes...I left earth just recently."

James laughed with what I can only describe as the friendliest chuckle I might have ever heard. He seemed very natural with people, and I immediately felt at ease.

"I'd like to say Mr. James, it is *such* an honor to meet you! I really enjoyed reading your book and learned so much."

"Oh the honor is mine, Danielle," he interrupted, modestly waving off my praise. "I'm glad you read my letter to the churches, but the truth is it was all the Holy Spirit's inspiration. So tell me. Did anything puzzle you in my letter? Some parts had very deep layers and required a deep relationship with the Holy Spirit to understand."

I thought about that for a second, and then realized I actually did have a question. When James mentioned the Holy Spirit again, it clicked for me. I tilted my head to the side in thought, and then began to talk. "In the Bible, Jesus says the Holy Spirit is our Comforter, but why is there so much sadness and loneliness among Christians?" Loneliness was one of the reasons I had been tempted to make unwise choices, and I knew from talking to my friends that it affected them too. The contrast between the loneliness on earth and the joyful, family-like environment here was extremely stark.

"Danielle, that's a great question."

I listened intently. He had a way of really drawing listeners in.

"On the simplest level, we don't have what we need because we don't ask."

I felt like slapping my palm to my forehead. That was straight out of his book. I knew the next part, "Or we ask and do not receive..." From his expression, he saw that I knew it, and raised his eyebrows, motioning for me to finish. "...because we ask amiss..."

He smiled, and everyone around looked impressed that I knew the scripture.

"We don't ask in line with God's will, right?" I added, feeling more confident.

"Exactly, my dear," he said enthusiastically. "The Holy Spirit will do His best to comfort those still running the race on earth, but He can only do great things with someone if they ask for His help, and *allow* Him to help."

"So...like...pray?" I asked, almost feeling silly again.

James threw his hands up in a way that showed his good-natured, Jewish character. "Of course." He laughed. "She's got it!" The others also laughed.

"So, we can ask the Holy Spirit to help us not be lonely, and He will bring us true, Christian friends?" I asked.

"Well...yes, He will because community and family are very important to God. But the Holy Spirit is also the best friend you can have on earth. He desires a strong, personal relationship with you as well."

I nodded again, letting this sink in. I realized Jesus' presence was so familiar to me because the Holy Spirit would speak to me and try to comfort me in the same way on earth. I suddenly wished I had devoted a lot more time getting to know Him.

"Why do we neglect our relationship with Him?" I asked James.

"Well, your spirit is strongly drawn to His voice, but many people are distracted by things of the world. The flesh can be a powerful deterrent. The enemy also works to suggest cheap substitutes for the Holy Spirit's presence." He paused for a second. "And many don't actually read God's Word like you did, Danielle. The Holy Spirit will enlighten the Word for you, and you will recognize His voice more clearly at the same time."

It all made a lot of sense now. I smiled at James and nodded.

"I wish I had learned how easy and important it is to ask for help on earth," I said. "It sure would help a lot of people down there."

Chapter Fourteen:

FORGIVENESS

I was sitting out on the deck one day reflecting on life and how things change. I thought back to the letter Danielle gave me on Mother's day, a week before the accident. One of her statements was: "Mom, thanks for being the greatest example in forgiveness. After making mistakes, you showed me so much love and care which helped so much." I thought, *Oh Danielle, those acts of forgiveness were nothing compared to what God is asking me to do right now.*

I didn't know the girls who had the party, and I honestly didn't blame them for the accident. However, I did realize they hosted the party where my daughter made some awful choices. She drank and then she drove. I could have continued to dwell on the fact that they had the party and didn't prevent her from driving, and these thoughts would have continued to torment me. There was a choice before me...I could choose to allow bitterness to enter my heart or choose to forgive. I asked God to change my heart, release any hurt that I was feeling, and help me to forgive.

A few months after the accident, I received an email from one of Danielle's Bethel friends. It was a girl I didn't know, but she talked about the positive influence Danielle had on her life. Then, out of the blue, she began apologizing profusely. She had been the one who invited Danielle to the party. It was apparent she was feeling unbearable torment and guilt. She ended the email with: "You should be proud of Danielle... she was an absolutely wonderful woman of God and truly impacted everyone she met."

I broke down crying. As I cried and prayed, I also realized that this precious girl had to be utterly broken for her to send an email to me, Danielle's mom, admitting she invited Danielle to the party. God had miraculously shown me how she, too, was suffering deeply. I emailed the girl back, extending forgiveness, then added, "Your gift to me and to Danielle would be to live for Jesus 100% realizing that our life here on earth is so brief."

I realize many of you are reading this and thinking, *You have no idea how badly someone has hurt me or hurt someone I love. There's no way I can forgive that person.* I am so sorry for how you are hurting right now. I agree, you can't forgive the person in your own strength, but I'm praying that you can go to God and rely on His grace to forgive the other. Forgiveness is not a feeling. It is a choice to tear up the record of wrongs we have been keeping.

I was interested in how others dealt with forgiveness when the offending act seemed even more random than Danielle's accident. As I read Sittser's book recounting his journey of forgiveness, I could feel the torment in his writing as he desperately wanted justice to be served upon the drunk driver who had robbed him of his mother, wife, and child. Justice, however, did not occur and the driver was acquitted. Subsequently, the unanswered desire for justice turned into a desire for revenge. Thanks to God, he ultimately realized he needed to forgive the driver or be consumed by bitterness. He chose forgiveness.

Forgiving is not easy because it is a conscious act to give up your desire to get even. Sittser says, "However difficult, forgiveness in the end brings freedom to the one who gives it. Forgiving people let God run the universe. They let God punish wrongdoers as He wills, and they let God show mercy as He wills too."[26]

When we refuse to forgive and we remain bitter, we delude ourselves into thinking that the other person is being hurt in our quest to punish them. The truth is, the one who refuses to forgive, who dwells on the offense, and fantasizes about what it will be like when the other is punished, is the one who is being hurt and loses out on peace. This is apparent in Beth Moore's testimony. She experienced significant trauma as a child, and truly understands how difficult it can be to forgive someone:

> God changed the way I looked at the entire situation when I began to see that my grudge against people who hurt me only strengthened the grip of my bondage to them. ...When we won't forgive, the people we often want to be around least because they've hurt us so badly are the very people we take with us emotionally everywhere we go.[27]

Now please understand, forgiveness doesn't mean you condone the wrong actions of others, nor are you excusing their behavior. You are simply giving it over to God, where it belongs. He will work out His justice. Forgiveness is obedience to God. We are told in Romans 12:9: "Do not take revenge, my friends, but leave room for God's wrath, for it is written: 'It is mine to avenge; I will repay,' says the Lord."

I know so many of you have been mistreated and have experienced significant pain. I also realize it is human nature to be angry, hold a grudge, and to seek revenge. I would encourage you to go to God and just be honest with Him. Tell God how you feel, and ask Him to help you to turn the hatred over to Him and give you the grace you need to forgive those who have hurt you or your loved ones. Allow God to release you from being tied to the people who have hurt you, by giving you the strength to forgive them. If your heart is saturated with unforgiveness and bitterness, you become victims of your own venom and it will rob your peace. That's not what God wants for your life. He wants you to experience complete peace and joy. It is possible when you forgive. Here's a sample prayer to forgive those who hurt you:

Lord Jesus, I am powerless to forgive. My flesh wants vengeance, yet I know it is Your will that I forgive. In the same manner that You have forgiven me of all my offenses, I choose right now to forgive _____. I release _____ into Your hands. I give up every "right" to harbor any resentment. Give me the grace to renew my mind as I refuse to dwell on the feelings of unforgiveness as they resurface. Bring my emotions into alignment with my choice to forgive. Guard my heart so that no root of bitterness can spring up. Thank You for Your enabling grace. In Jesus name, Amen.

———◈———

While I was waiting for Jesus to come back, I was still sort of star-struck as I sat talking to James and his students. James and one of the men began talking about the deeper mechanisms of why we need to ask for help. It was getting very complicated, so I zoned out a bit. A lovely young woman next to me had long, raven-black hair, warm brown eyes, and wore a pretty light-blue scarf draped around her head. She was clearly from a time that occurred a long time ago. Maybe she sensed my distraction because she started chatting to me.

After a few minutes of chatting, she asked, "I perceive you left earth quite young. How did you come to be here?" I realized that our conversation had caught the attention of James and the others. They had stopped talking and were also waiting for my response.

"Well...I was at a party...a...celebration and..." I paused for a second. James shook his head slightly and dismissed the slight awkwardness I felt with his eyes. In a glance he said, "It's okay, we've all made mistakes. It's all done with."

"I drank too much alcohol, and was really tired, and got in a car accident."

My new friend looked at James for clarification and he said, "It's like a chariot...but runs without horses, and can go many times the speed of a horse." She raised her eyebrows.

"So no one made sure you could operate your vehicle?" he asked.

"Well sort of. I said I was fine..."

Everyone had become quiet. There was absolutely no judgment from the group, but it was a moment with many overtones.

"I don't blame my friends at all. It was really my choice," I said.

"I know, Danielle," James said quickly.

"I really hope my family understands though. It must be hard for them."

"Indeed," he said, and everyone around us nodded. "The Holy Spirit will continuously work to comfort and guide them to the path of healing," he continued. "But I'm sure they are tempted to harbor anger toward those who encouraged you to make wrong decisions. Forgiveness is one of the most difficult milestones to master in the race. Our Lord places a critical requirement on forgiveness."

"What do you mean?" I asked.

"When our Lord was crucified, it was the most horrific contrast you've ever seen."

I remembered only then that he had been there, and a wave of awe and emotion washed over me. The memory was obviously a very deep part of him.

"To see an innocent Lamb being slandered, spat upon, beaten...murdered. And by common brutes and organized religious criminals. Those of us who were there remember that day vividly. We watched in horror as our Lord was arrested, condemned as a criminal...condemned to death, shamed as a criminal, flogged, and a cursed crown of thorns placed upon His righteous head. He was beaten again, and again, and again. Yet He carried His cross with strength forged by the knowledge He was saving those who were crying for Him. While bitter, sarcastic, hateful words spewed from on-lookers, the religious elite who were supposed to be the example taunted and mocked, 'Come down from the cross if you are the Son of God! He saved others but He can't save Himself.'

We watched our Lord Jesus with a broken body, wracked with pain, eyes blinded by His own blood, and lungs yearning for air. He struggled to breathe. I was beside myself as I watched him take every excrutiating breath while trying to pull Himself up for air with His torn hands.

"Yet we heard no anger. No bitterness...only forgiveness. The first words out of His mouth in the face of this heinous injustice were ones of love, yet this was not the most difficult part." The memory clearly brought deep emotion within him...but surprisingly it was joyful, and without pain.

"The most difficult part," James continued, "was when He cleaned the slate for us. It was almost unfathomable."

"Wow!" I said. I was tingling all over. "I watched a movie called *Passion Of The Christ*, and it was horrible to watch. I'm sure the real thing was much worse."

James nodded. "I have heard of this re-enactment, and it sounds close to what happened. Our precious Jesus just said 'Father, forgive them.'" Everyone nodded agreement and all murmured praises.

"How could He do that?" I asked in astonishment.

"Indeed," James said. "The stakes were extremely high. The price was steep."

I was absolutely amazed. I couldn't imagine forgiving someone who was intentionally torturing and killing me.

"But how did He do that?" I asked again.

"Well, first, He didn't do it from an emotional basis. Forgiveness is not a feeling; it's an act of the will. Jesus forgave in obedience to His Father." He paused to let that sink in for a few seconds.

"Also, remember that Jesus is the embodiment of God's love. He wanted every one of His enemies to be able to turn from their wickedness and ignorance and join Him in Paradise. They really didn't know what they were doing, and several of them were saved in later years because of His act of forgiveness."

"Whew..." I said under my breath. This was amazing stuff. "I really hope my family is able to forgive."

"The Holy Spirit is very persuasive, my child." James smiled.

This really warmed my heart. I loved this father in the faith so much already. He was so wise.

"One last thing...with great sacrifice comes great reward. As in the case of our Lord, when He forgave such heinous crimes, it opened the way for us to join Him in eternal life!"

The tingles hit me again...and it was glorious!

"That's amazing! Hallelujah!" I shouted.

"HALLELUJAH!" our group echoed and the praised rippled down the steps, all the way through the crowd. No one needed a second invitation to praise our mighty King! I laughed loudly and everyone joined in.

"Oh look! He is coming back," my new friend with the blue scarf said, pointing to one of the incoming golden streets. There were already roars of praise, and melodies of bells and chimes and strings breaking out.

"Woohoo!" I yelled and everyone laughed again.

"My name is Rebekah, Danielle. It is so wonderful to meet you!" She gave me a warm hug.

"Oh, likewise Rebekah! You're absolutely gorgeous, by the way!"

"Ha ha...thank you! As are you, young lady."

I was so happy to be making such fascinating new friends. I was even happier that my Lord was making His way back to me.

Suddenly I remembered something, "Oh Rebekah, one more thing..." I began.

"Yes?" she replied, curiously.

"What does *Simcha* mean in English?"

A wide smile crossed her face as she realized why I was asking. "It means 'joy,' Danielle!"

Joy! After all that, Mom and I got my guardian angel's name right. I squeezed her hand again, and looked over to my Lord as He got closer.

Chapter Fifteen:

In Light Of Eternity

———∞∞∞———

S ometimes I feel like May 17th, 2008 was a "wake-up knock," similar to a wake-up call. I slept through an alarm years ago while traveling for business and the consequences weren't fun. I learned the hard way that I need wake-up calls so I don't miss something important. For me, the wake-up knock on May 17th (when I was awakened by the sound of the police officer knocking on the door) was a significant reminder of the brevity of life and the importance of sharing my faith with others. Sleeping through this wake-up knock would have had eternal consequences—for myself and for others impacted by Danielle's story.

C.S. Lewis wrote, "pain is God's megaphone to a deaf world." Pain can serve as a wake-up call for people. One of the most dangerous things we can do, if God is allowing pain as a megaphone, is to go back to sleep. Jesus really loves us and may allow loss and hardship to show us our need for a Savior.

If you died today, are you sure you would go to Heaven?

Yes, you *can* know for sure that you are going to Heaven! We were created to have a relationship with God both now and forever. Because of sin, our fellowship with God was broken. He bridged the gap which separates us from Him by sending His Son, Jesus Christ, to die on the cross to pay the penalty for our sins. This is the most important decision we will ever make—to recognize that we have sinned, to make a decision to put our total trust in Jesus to forgive our sins, and to choose to follow Him. John 3:16 speaks to the wonderful truth of God's love for us: "God so loved the world that He gave His one and only Son, that whoever believes in Him shall not perish but have eternal life."

This has *eternal importance* so please hear me. If there has never been a time that you've trusted Jesus Christ as your only basis of forgiveness, please let this be the day and don't put off making that choice.

Now, I want to take a moment and talk to the person who is struggling because you do not have assurance of where your loved one who died is right now. We simply cannot know what happens inside a person before they die. We don't know whether the Holy Spirit has done a work of grace in someone's heart at the last moment. God may have brought to their memory aspects of the Gospel that had been shared with them. Unbeknownst to you, they may have privately turned to Christ in faith, and you will be delighted someday to see them in Heaven. If you are unsure whether a last-minute decision can be accepted, read the account of Jesus' conversation with the thief hanging on the cross beside him (Luke 23:38-43).

Danielle's early homegoing has served to help me discover depths of spiritual blessings I really only hoped I could grasp this side of eternity. For that, I am so grateful. And there is no greater gift Danielle could have left me than the assurance that she loved Jesus and is now with Him for eternity. In light of these things, I have unshakable hope and joyful expectation about eternity.

God has wasted nothing here. He has now perfected Danielle's joy. And He's growing mine.

───── ⋙⋘ ─────

My precious Lord made His way through the crowd of His beloved people and up the steps toward me. Walking next to Him, grinning broadly, was Simcha. It still impressed me how huge the angel was, and with such a kind, but resolute face.

He truly was a warrior of light. Extremely formidable, but only as a warrior of the King and protector of His children. The mind-blowing thing was that I then realized Jesus is the Commander-In-Chief over legions and legions of these warriors. It made His voluntary sacrifice that much more astounding.

"Danielle! I missed your smile!" Jesus grinned as He hugged me.

"Oh Lord Jesus, I felt Your presence with me the entire time!" I hugged Him as if I would never let Him go.

"You are correct my sweet child. But I still love seeing you, first-hand." He laughed. The atmosphere in Heaven is indescribably wonderful, but when Jesus is right there, it's off the charts. James and the others were also standing in reverence, and the Lord leaned over and hugged James, smiling a greeting. "Brother."

"Lord." James bowed his head slightly.

Jesus patted the rest of the group on their shoulders.

"Simcha!" I squealed, and hugged him too. It was evident that angels were never discriminated against, but were clearly subject to the children of God. I didn't want him to feel left out and, of course, he didn't. He was still my buddy.

"You've been enjoying yourself?" the Lord asked.

"Oh wow, yes!" I laughed. "James is so full of wisdom."

Jesus nodded and raised His eyebrows, concurring.

"She's a very astute handmaiden, my Lord," James said sincerely.

"Isn't she just?" The Lord smiled again, putting His elbow around my neck and pulling me into Him. "This one has already left quite the legacy in her few years in the race. Danielle, I have a little task you may be able to help me with, if I may ask," Jesus added in a humble tone. His humility was still mind-blowing, considering He was the King of Heaven.

"Oh, my Lord, anything at all," I said, bowing my head. I was excited to hear what He was going to ask of me.

"Well, there are some new graduates who have spent almost no time on earth." I wondered for a second what

He meant, and then I realized He was talking about *babies*! I was very intrigued. I had always known babies graduated straight to Heaven, as they hadn't reached their individual age of accountability, and therefore hadn't yet had to choose to accept or reject the Savior.

"You are quite adept in the knowledge of my Word. Perhaps you could guide them through the basics of how My Kingdom works?"

I was amazed. I didn't feel qualified, but if the Lord said I could do it, I knew I could. And I would be working with babies! I loved babies! Suddenly it dawned on me that I had a job! Commissioned by my Savior—and it was absolutely wonderful!

"I would be honored, my Lord!" I squeaked, jumping up and down and clapping my hands. Everyone laughed at my enthusiasm. Even Simcha chuckled.

"Danielle, would you mind if Simcha escorted you back to your house, where your eager students are waiting?"

"No, of course not," I said. I was already thinking about what I would be teaching those babies. And how much would they understand?

Jesus, of course, anticipated my questions and said, "Simcha will help you understand your task with the young ones." I nodded and smiled eagerly again. "Brethren," Jesus said, turning to James and the group, "thank you for sharing your time with Danielle."

"Our pleasure, Lord," said James with a quick, small bow, speaking for the group. The others also nodded and bowed slightly.

"Wonderful to meet you Danielle!" Rebekah said, hugging me warmly.

"Oh, the pleasure is mine," I said squeezing Rebekah's hands. For a moment, I didn't want to leave. The feeling was instantly replaced by an eagerness to move on to the next adventure. I knew I would visit my new friends again, soon enough.

"Simcha, I will see you soon," the Lord said, revealing something in His statement that made me thoughtful. Simcha bowed slightly and gave a small, reverential nod displaying submission and pure love in the same gesture.

I gave Jesus one last, big hug and then waved my goodbyes to my new friends as Simcha and I turned to leave. Apparently my Lord was staying with James and his group for a little while. Simcha and I walked back down the stepped structure. I was in awe again at how the beautiful design changed shapes and form as I walked by, seeing it from differing perspectives. Everything in Heaven was just pure art—incomprehensible genius in its creation.

Simcha turned and grinned at me, like the old friend he was. "Are you excited about your assignment?"

"For real!" I replied. "So what am I going to be teaching the precious babies?"

"Well, they are aware of the Lord's glory and His kingship. And, of course, they don't have much *unlearning* to do." Simcha paused for a second as that last line sank in.

It made sense. I came here with many preconceived notions and had been pretty surprised already at how different things were in Heaven—from how I imagined them. *Better* different.

"But...If I had to take a guess...they haven't really had a need to understand His sacrifice and work of atonement? Right?"

"Precisely," Simcha replied. "But even before that, they would do well to firmly grasp the significance of obedience." He took a moment and then clarified, "They'll never know disobedience, but so they can frame the wonders of His work, perhaps start with the story of your ancestors, Adam and Eve. They love story time." He smiled.

Oh, I was so excited. This was going to be *fun*!

"And you're sure I'll be up to the task?" I said.

"You're up it," he explained, "or you wouldn't be assigned." Then his thoughts seemed to trail off.

I nodded with a look that said, "Yeah, I guess so, huh?"

We had now left the square and were walking down a golden street parallel to the one on which I walked up with Jesus. The houses in this row were Victorian-looking, but even more majestic. I took it all in as children playing tag waved as we walked by. Simcha and I waved back at the same moment. He smiled and I sensed his thoughts going distant again.

"So what about you?" I asked him.

"What about me?" he echoed, halfway dodging the question.

"You're going to help me teach the babies, right?" He took a moment and then looked down at the ground.

"Only for a moment," he said turning his eyes to mine. "You could probably tell, the Lord has a new assignment for me." My heart dropped a little. I had really bonded with this cool angel and to this point, I hadn't really thought about how he might not just hang out with me indefinitely.

"Here in Heaven?" I asked, but I already knew the answer. He just smiled halfheartedly and shook his head.

"No, I'm off to watch over a little boy about to be born," Sincha said softly. "Apparently he has a very special purpose."

I nodded. I was disappointed, but not sad. I understood that it all was in the plan of God, and I would see Simcha again before I knew it. The great news was that eternity was a long time, and even a lifetime on earth was a breath in Heaven.

"Neat!" I said. He smiled and nodded. "I'll miss you," I said honestly.

"I'll miss you too, Danielle," he said, smiling with his eyes. "But I'll see you before too long. You will find that you'll be so busy enjoying yourself, it will be like a blink before I see you again."

"Can't wait!" I said, and our thoughts hung in the silence for a second. "Oh look! There are children at my house!" I changed the subject quickly.

"Yes. Those are your students."

"I thought they were babies!"

"Their earth-bodies were those of infants, but here they begin their journey with more practical bodies."

"Wow," I said. Again, these concepts were pretty new. Somehow it all made sense. The children appeared to be playing hide and seek in the garden. It looked like such fun, I wanted to join in!

We walked up to the gate, and a blonde lady with the sweetest face greeted us. "Simcha!" she said holding her arms out. She was really excited to see him.

"Margaret." He grinned and hugged her tightly. Simcha turned to me and said,

"Margaret, this is Danielle. Another outstanding daughter of the Lord."

I smiled, wondering how they knew each other.

"Oh what a pleasure to meet you Danielle! I was told these precious children would be in the finest of hands." Margaret was just adorable. She had the kindest eyes and a warm, sincere air about her.

"Oh, thank you." I smiled at her, instantly liking her tremendously.

"Simcha is a dear friend to me, as I know he is to you," she said, with an inflection of added meaning in her voice.

I realized at that point Simcha had been her guardian too. This was really great, as I now had a glimpse of what it would be like when I saw my friend again.

"Margaret is going to get you started with the guidance of the children," Simcha said.

"Wonderful!" I nodded. I was glad for the help.

"Precious ones!" Margaret called out. "Come and meet my friend Danielle!"

The children who were hiding popped out of some leaves and from behind a willow tree, and the others squealed with laughter. They all scampered over to us.

"Whoa! You're huge!" one of the little boys said, gazing up at Simcha. The angel laughed and went to one knee to pat the little guy on the head.

"If you listen carefully to Margaret and Danielle, you might be even bigger and stronger, young man!" Simcha said.

The boy's eyes widened and immediately a look of determination crossed his face. I knew he would listen resolutely to every word we spoke. We laughed together again and Simcha ruffled his hair.

"Aren't you guys just precious!" I also got down on their level. I counted twelve of them elbowing around us. They all grinned like Cheshire cats. One little girl sidled up next to me and took my hand in hers. She had long, curly blonde locks. Some were braided into a little crown around her head. Others went down the back in a French braid. She was just the sweetest thing!

"What's your name, gorgeous girl?" I asked.

"Heather," she replied shyly, trilling the "r" in the cutest little Scottish accent. She squeezed my hand tighter and inched even closer, pressing right in to my side.

"Heather! That's so pretty!" I squeezed her.

"What's your name?" a little boy from India blurted out.

"I told you, Abhi," Margaret said. "Her name is Danielle. She's your new teacher."

"Ohh," Abhi said thoughtfully. "I like her!" he then proclaimed.

"I like her too!" a few others echoed. "So do I! So do I!" They started jumping up and down around me and a few began grappling with Heather for one of my hands. I laughed giddily at these sweet kiddos. They were just too precious. Margaret and Simcha were also chuckling at the jostling little mob of joy.

After they settled down, Simcha said, "Okay, dear children, do you want to go and play for a bit more? Simcha has to talk to Margaret and Danielle for a little while."

"Okay!" they chorused, and a few gave my legs one last, emphatic hug before they dashed off. I couldn't wait to start hanging out with them.

Simcha sighed with a small smile that said, "I suppose it's time."

"Oh, Simcha, I pray I don't see you for a lifetime, but can't wait until I see you again!" I threw my arms around the big teddy bear's chest. He returned the hug, bowed his head down and rested his cheek on my head.

"I'll miss you too, wonderful Danielle. I'm so glad you're safe and sound for eternity."

I looked up at him, and although I didn't want to cry, my emotions were running pretty high. "Thank you for all you've done for me."

He nodded and said, "All in the King's service, my dear. Thank you for the honor of serving a true handmaiden of the Lord."

I marveled at the consistent humility of this messenger for the Lord.

"Well...without further ado..."

I smiled again. An angel with Shakespearean vocabulary.

"So good to see you!" Simcha hugged Margaret tightly. "We'll spend more time together the next time around."

"Ah, Simcha, you champion!" She smiled. "Go and fulfill your task and make the great God Jehovah even more proud."

"Praise His holy name," Simcha said and bowed slightly.

"Praise His holy name," we both repeated.

"Right then..." the great warrior said. "I'll be seeing you." After putting a hand on each of our shoulders, he turned and began walking back in the direction of the pearl gates.

We watched him for a while and waved when he turned around at the summit of the first hill. He waved back and we could see his big, kind smile even from a way off. As he disappeared behind the horizon, we both suddenly sensed a familiar, glorious presence. At the same moment, the children discarded their game and darted for the front of the garden. I spun around and squeaked with joy as I saw our Savior walking up the path.

"Jesus! Jesus!" The children swarmed Him. He bent down and scooped up the first two who made it to Him, and laughed loudly as He bounced them in each arm while He walked. The children were going wild; some were jumping around like little pogo sticks and others dashing around His legs madly. It was hilarious. Margaret and I were laughing so hard at the sight. The truth was, we could barely restrain ourselves from joining them. Jesus' presence was just so magnificent.

"Margaret! Danielle!" He laughed as the two in His arms clung to Him, refusing to be put down.

"Lord!" We returned the greeting, laughing in unison.

"To what do we owe this pleasure, Lord?" Margaret wrestled one of the children off His arm and set her on the ground.

"I wanted to see how Danielle was enjoying her first assignment." He looked at me and smiled.

"Oh Lord, these children are just beautiful!" I said. "I can't wait to begin sharing with them."

"Wonderful," He said. "Your friend, Simcha, has left?"

"Yes, my Lord. Right before You arrived."

"Good. Good." He smiled. "He has an important task ahead of him. He'll face some real opposition, but he will fulfill his duty like the warrior of Light that he is."

I nodded.

Margaret must have sensed Jesus had something to discuss with me, because she said, "I'm going to get the little ones inside and try to settle them down."

"Thank you, Margaret," Jesus said, acknowledging her graciousness.

"Who wants to see Danielle's snowboard room?" Margaret called out to the children.

They started bouncing around again and a few called out "Woohoo!" I giggled as I watched them scamper after Margaret, into the house.

"You're settling in well, my dear?" Jesus asked, taking my hand and beginning to walk toward the front garden.

"Oh yes." I smiled. "If I had known this is how my eternal home would be, I would have worked even harder for Your Kingdom!"

Jesus nodded, looking at the ground as we walked. "Many say that. Yes, I think a large number of My children don't realize how short their race on earth really is." He looked up at me and smiled. I wished I could take a picture of His smile and His face and show the world. "Do you miss your family?"

"In a way," I said. "I really look forward to being reunited with them. I want them to experience this joy, but I know in my heart they still have their races to run."

He looked at me proudly and squeezed my hand. We were near the rose bushes now. He picked a large cerise-colored rose and gave it to me. I sniffed it and a fragrance that no perfume on earth could ever match filled my senses.

"That is beautiful!" I said, and took another huge breath of it. It was *invigorating*. Then I realized something interesting. "No thorns!" I loved roses, but I knew one had to be careful when handling a rose just picked. There were almost always thorns covering the stem.

"Ah yes. No thorns here!" Jesus said. "The curse that brought thorns to earth does not exist here. There is no sin."

I sighed and shook my head, pondering the price He paid for us, so we could spend eternity in a home where sin does not exist.

"Lord?" I began.

"Yes, my dear?"

"Is my family going to be okay?" We had discussed it a little, but I wanted to know more about how they were doing. "I know they are strong, but they haven't seen Heaven. I know how difficult it can be on earth."

"Oh, I wouldn't say they haven't seen Heaven. Your mom has definitely glimpsed Heaven in her prayers...even through her tears."

"Really?" I asked.

"Oh, yes. Remember, everyone on earth is a spirit being, living in a body," He began to explain. "Through My Spirit, I gave your mom a touch from Heaven. The night of the accident, she really needed to know you were okay, and I wanted her to experience my indescribable peace—even in the middle of her terrible pain."

I thought about this. I didn't want my mom to suffer, but I knew she would get through it. I remembered the one thing my mom clung to was the Word of God. And *that* was the best thing she could do.

"What about Ashley and Nathan?" I asked. "How are they doing?"

"Danielle, part of My continuing work is to intercede for all believers. I present all of your family to My Father without ceasing. And My Spirit is constantly working in their hearts, comforting them, guiding them through the pain."

I nodded. This gave me extreme hope and joy. The Father, Son and Spirit were a mind-bogglingly powerful force.

"Your family and loved ones all have their own choices to make. And, yes, their perceived loss of you is a trial that is changing their lives. This, like all suffering, is an opportunity for them to grow closer to Me. Your family has to work through some deep and challenging matters. I am loving them and waiting while they learn to make choices in obedience— choices that will ultimately make them stronger and happier."

"Can't You just...*make* them understand what awesome joy is available to them?" I asked. I really didn't want my family to have to suffer. "Wouldn't it be easier if they just understood why this happened, and how happy I am right now?"

"Ah yes, this is one of the deeper mysteries of my kingdom," He said. "Revelation and understanding always come through obedience. For example, remember when I told my twelve that the greatest in the Kingdom of God is the servant of all?"

"Yes," I replied, recalling a verse that I loved.

"I came to earth as a humble servant, yes?"

I nodded, as it still amazed me every time I thought about it.

"Obedient to My Father, even to the point of torture and death?"

I nodded again slowly. A revelation was slowly coming together in my mind.

"Submission is one of the keys to My kingdom," He said, making sure I was grasping the full implication of what He was saying. "Wisdom and knowledge comes from submission and obedience."

"Wow!" I said, suddenly grasping the full realization and sorting through it in my mind. "So that's why we only *fully* understand something *after* we've been obedient first?"

Jesus nodded and gave me that smile that said, "You've got it!"

He continued, "And one of the greatest tests of all is obedience in the face of terrible tragedy and pain. When injustice seems to engulf you, but you remain obedient—this is the sign of a highly mature believer, capable of great victories for My Kingdom."

"My family is going to do great things for Your Kingdom, aren't they, Lord?"

"Yes, they are, Danielle." Jesus smiled at me. "They are suffering, but I am refining them. Even in the middle of their perceived tragedy, My Spirit consoles them and encourages them to remain faithful. And they are overcoming, sometimes when they don't even realize it."

His words filled me with so much joy and peace and excitement. I was simply marveling at the work of my Lord. I knew He had my family in the palm of His hand. My family would do wonderful things for His Kingdom and join me here when their race was done. Jesus put His strong arm around my shoulder and we continued to walk through the lush garden He had given me.

"Thank You, my Lord," I said. I was truly so grateful that I had such a loving, brilliant God. "You are so good, and wonderful. I love You with all of my heart!" I said as I threw my arms around His neck and buried my head in His shoulder.

Finally He took me by the shoulders and looked into my eyes. "I'll never leave them, nor forsake them—just as I never left you. I promise."

I was overcome with emotion and all I could manage was, "I'm certain of that, my Lord."

He took my hand again and we kept walking. I breathed in deeply and then exhaled. Jesus' presence was exhilarating.

"What are you doing after you teach those kiddos their first lesson?" Jesus asked.

"I hadn't really thought of it." I smiled up at Him, getting excited again. I was really looking forward to teaching and playing with those sweet children.

"The river runs through a beautiful grove of fruit trees just beyond the next hill." He pointed to the right of my house, the opposite direction from the pearl gates. "You and Margaret may want to take them on a picnic."

"That's a great idea!" I said. "A river? Can we swim in it?"

"Oh yes. I strongly recommend it," Jesus said, grinning broadly again. "You should also drink from it. I think you'll find it quite energizing."

Then it hit me. "The River of Life?" I cried out then looked at Him for confirmation. He nodded, still grinning.

"Woohoo!" I jumped up and yelped like one of the kids. "That's going to be awesome!" I said.

Jesus laughed loudly and appeared to always thoroughly enjoy it when I was excited.

"Danielle, I have to go now but I'll come back and see how you're doing soon."

"Oh, okay Lord. You can't join us for the picnic?"

"I'm with you *always*, dear. You've already been experiencing the joy of my presence in countless ways. Come swing by the city square any time, and I'll meet you again this way there. I will also let your family know they could meet us there."

"Oh Lord, I love You so much." I hugged Him again and He lifted me off my feet and spun me around.

"I love you too, my child!" He smiled. "Go and enjoy those children, and get them up to speed on the good things I have in store for them!"

"I will make You proud!"

"You already have, my faithful servant."

I smiled from ear to ear.

"Lord Jesus?" I asked, almost forgetting a question that had been on my mind since I went to the city square.

"Yes, Danielle."

"Will I be meeting my Heavenly Father?"

Jesus smiled and His eyes lit up even more. I could tell my enthusiasm to meet my Father brought Him a lot of joy.

"Yes, my sweet Danielle...and that will be an unparalleled experience for you." His eyes shone as He thought of it. I trembled with excitement. I couldn't wait to meet the One who loved me so much that He sent His precious Son to die for me!

His gaze lingered on me for a moment, then He gave me the most adoring smile. He turned and began walking back down to the road.

"Oh and about your family..." He shouted back. "I'll keep you posted on the work they're doing for Me!" Jesus waved as He continued walking.

That was my Lord. Always leaving something to look forward to. I stood for a second as I watched my precious Savior walk back up toward His royal City—a city full of glorious people who adored Him with every good reason. And He adored them. The surge of joy in my heart lifted me off my feet as I considered how the rest of eternity would be with Him in this Paradise.

That was worth getting super-excited about.

Appendix:

ADVANCING TOWARD JOY

—∞∞—

M any of you are in a dark season of life and you are experiencing days of tears, anger, and sadness. I know it is not easy and I am so sorry that you are hurting. This section offers practical advice on grief and loss, drawing upon my counseling experience as well as my own personal walk through the valley of shadows. It is my prayer that this information will provide a frame of reference from which to understand your own grief and help you move toward hope and joy.

Grief Spiral

Every person's grief is unique, yet there are some typical phases. These phases are often referred to as a *grief spiral* because people will move back and forth among them, sometimes even vacillating between several phases in a single day. People may feel like they should be experiencing grief in a predictable, linear fashion. Instead, grief is erratic. Good moments can frequently be interrupted by difficult moments. The unpredictable timing of these emotions can leave a person very confused. It's difficult to feel that healing is taking place at all when you find yourself on an emotional roller coaster. The phases described below are based on the work of Parkes[28] and Sanders.[29]

Phase One: Shock, Numbness, and Denial

The first phase of grief is the initial period of shock, numbness, and denial. When I received the news of Danielle's death, I felt stunned and overwhelmed. There was an initial sense of disbelief, but as reality began to take hold, the pain was simply crushing. I was very confused the first few days, as I vacillated between numbness and unspeakable agony.

The numbness has been described as "a buffer, allowing the mourner to absorb the reality of the loss gradually over time and serving as emotional anesthesia while the mourner begins to experience the painful awareness of the loss."[30] This profoundly disconcerting period is when we're struggling to face what seems unthinkable.

When we are in shock, we may be unable to think coherently. At some point during that first night, the phone rang and it was someone who needed my permission to donate Danielle's organs. I could barely comprehend what they were saying. What I didn't realize at the time is that a grieving person is going through an extremely traumatic experience which leaves us exhausted and weak, both physically and mentally.

Denial is a natural response that gives us time to grasp reality. I remember waking up a number of times over the first few days thinking I had experienced a horrible nightmare, only to realize the nightmare was reality. Early in the grief cycle, it is fairly common to recognize, on an intellectual level, that the triggering event has occurred while, on another level, not believe it is true. Sometimes you feel like you are going crazy. A week after the accident, everyone had left the house and no one was expected home soon. Suddenly I heard the garage door and the door to the house opened. A surge of excitement went through me and I went running to the kitchen to hug Danielle only to see my Mom standing there. I just broke down and cried. For a moment, it really felt like Danielle was back.

Denial may be helpful for a short period of time because we are not ready to confront the loss directly and fully. Ultimately, we do need to move through denial into the difficult reality of the loss to begin the grieving process. We need to see the loss as something that cannot be reversed. In order for me to heal, I needed to accept the fact that Danielle had died and I would not see her again until our wonderful reunion in Heaven.

Grief can be utterly immobilizing during the early phases, so it's of critical importance to have a support network who can help us face what we are experiencing.

Phase Two: Yearning and Protesting

The second phase of grief is a period of yearning and protesting. This is what happens when a person deeply longs for the loved one to return but, in recognition of this impossibility, experiences a surge of feelings such as extreme sadness, fear, anger, blame and guilt.

Protesting is an intense emotional reaction to a painful experience. You hate what has happened and you desperately want to reverse it. My own spirit would groan with objections but it was important for me to work through that pain. The emotions were very perplexing. I could be handling life just fine when, all of a sudden, a wave of grief would engulf me and I would break down crying.

Sometimes individuals struggle with exhibiting their emotions and allowing the tears to flow. Norm Wright, who experienced a number of losses with a son who was severely disabled and who also died at a young age, says, "When words fail, tears are the messenger. Tears are God's gift to all of us to release our feelings."[31]

A very natural part of protesting is also vehemently asking, "Why?" King David, in the book of Psalms, often describes sorrowful questioning. "My God, my God, why have you forsaken me? Why are you so far from saving me, so far from my cries of anguish?" (Psalms 22:1)

One has to be careful, however, because I have personally spoken with many individuals who get stuck in this stage of their grief because of the unanswered "Why?" question. This prevents them from moving on toward healing and can result in long-term feelings of resentment, bitterness, anger, and despair. I understand the need to search for answers. However, as limited as our understanding often is, we have to resign ourselves to the fact that many of our questions will go unanswered on this earth. These mysteries are difficult to release. It often requires taking a step of faith.

Anger is a very common reaction during this phase, and often accompanies an impulse to place blame on someone, even yourself. You may be angry with someone who hurt you or a loved one. You may be angry with yourself for not being the perfect spouse, parent, son, or daughter. You may be angry with circumstances that are out of your control. You may be angry with God.

As I mentioned earlier, Jerry Sittser and his family were involved in a terrible car accident with a drunk driver. The accident caused the deaths of his wife, daughter, and mother. In his book, Jerry openly talks about being viciously angry with the man who had killed his loved ones, and also being angry with God. "At times I scoffed at the vain notion of praying to God or, conversely, of cursing God, as if one or the other would make any difference. At other times I cried out to God in utter anguish of soul, 'How could you do this to innocent people?'"[32]

Jerry eventually realized that these emotions were natural responses to loss, and he was able to reconcile with the Lord, Who ultimately healed him. During your dark hour of grief, please hang on to the fact that God profoundly loves you and wants you to cry out to Him with your anger, grief, doubts, and questions.

It is also possible to become angry with family or friends, feeling you aren't receiving the support you need. Instead of getting frustrated, try to look at this as a cue that you need to ask for support. Often when we are consumed by our grief, we assume others know what we need. Try to understand that they may not know when or how to comfort you.

Feel your anger, acknowledge it, and know that it is a normal part of the grieving process. Holding it in can lead to depression, so I would encourage you to find a safe way to express your anger. If you feel you are stuck, ask yourself, "Have I forgiven this person?" Unforgiveness will produce bitterness and hinder you from moving forward.

Fear and anxiety are also typical feelings that result from the grief experience. The world around us often feels less safe in the wake of a death or other tragedy. Anxiety can stem from feelings of helplessness or fear that you cannot get along by yourself. It is easy to get stuck in negative rehearsals where we look ahead and imagine the worst in a situation that has not even occurred. Typically, the fears and anxiety will pass; fears that persist may indicate deeper problems that may require counseling.

Guilt and self-blame can plague a person during this time. A grieving person must be on guard for the dangerous "black hole" of guilt that sucks a person further and further into destructive ways of thinking. You may experience regret for words said or unsaid, things done or not done. The "What if?" or "If only..." scenarios are common, and surface intensely in cases of sudden death. You may wonder if different actions on your part could have prevented the loss. You may even feel cheated of the opportunity to make amends for some wrongdoing. However, allowing these thoughts and feelings to linger only perpetuates ongoing guilt which will undoubtedly prevent healing.

Guilt can be an absolute killer if you keep beating yourself up, thinking perhaps you could have done things differently and prevented the loss. Often when we are grieving, our thoughts are not objective. If you are unable to stop blaming yourself it may help to see a counselor or pastor who can help you give your guilt a reality test. Quite often, guilt is irrational. Working with someone may help you to determine that there really was nothing that you could have done to change the outcome. Even if you have done things wrong, healing will come as you forgive yourself and release what might have been.

Regret is common, particularly with a sudden death. There have been many times I have just ached for the chance to say goodbye and tell Danielle how much I loved her. I can relate to the description Delores Kuenning writes:

> The impact of sudden death is devastating, for it happens without warning or a chance to anticipate what lies ahead. It allows no time for goodbyes, no time to make amends or ask forgiveness for harsh words spoken in trivial quarrels, and no time

to express the love one feels but doesn't verbalize. The unfinished business of the day can never be transacted—it remains unresolved. It is like an unfinished song, the melody stopped in mid-phrase that longs for completion.[33]

I'm so thankful that my last time with Danielle was so precious. I remember the conversations we had that day, the gleam in her eye when she handed me her Mother's Day letter, the tears she shed as I read the letter that expressed her love. And that last hug! I have played that memory over and over in my mind. But I still had so much I wanted to tell her.

Nathan had a similar regret and struggled with not having the chance to say goodbye. Shortly after the accident, I walked into his room where he was sitting on his bed. Between the deep sobs, and with a shaky voice, he said, "Mom, I didn't say goodbye to Danielle." I put my arms around him and joined him in crying. I asked him if he wanted to tell Jesus what he would like to say to Danielle. He nodded and had a sweet conversation with Jesus.

I was fortunate that my last day with Danielle on this earth was such a special day. There were many other days in our lives where our last encounter would not have been so positive, and there may have been more regret. Whether we lament the tone of our very last encounter with a loved one or something of other days gone by, it is helpful to settle on the positive memories. If your last memory of a loved one is unpleasant or if you are plagued with thoughts of regret, this advice from Norm Wright in his book, *Recovering From the Losses of Life,* may be helpful:

> Sometimes these last unpleasant scenes tend to haunt a person. Your task then will be to soften the memories and images that hurt you so much by doing some editing as if it were a movie. You can hang on to the hurting, negative images or choose to go back a bit further in time and dwell on a scene

that is representative of your relationship or how you feel about that person overall. Let that scene be your source of comfort.[34]

Unexpressed feelings can also significantly hinder the healing process. As painful as it may be, it is important to enter the darkness and grieve because avoiding grief only brings more issues later in your life.

At times, the reality that Danielle is gone has pierced right through my heart, and I have been overwhelmed with emotion. I have needed to know that I could cry out to God, "Father, I can't handle this pain!" It is helpful reading the Psalms and intentionally reminding myself of God's promises. One of my favorites is Psalm 34:18: "The LORD is close to the broken-hearted and saves those who are crushed in spirit."

New dimensions of loss is an often overlooked, but significant, and continuous reason for the roller coaster ride of grief. Not only was I reacting to the loss of Danielle, but also to secondary losses. Examples of secondary losses are the unfulfilled hopes and dreams, the special source of love and joy I received from Danielle, as well as the loss of part of my identity as Danielle's mom. Being Danielle's mom was one of my most valued roles in life. In one instant that role was eliminated. I still think of myself as Danielle's mom but, of course, it's different now. I have had to form a new understanding of myself that integrates the loss of Danielle into it.

A few weeks after the accident, I had a doctor's appointment and she asked me how many children I had. I froze, not knowing how to respond to that question. Finally I answered, with tears streaming down my face, "I have three children; two live with me and one is in Heaven." That is a question that I can still become emotional over, even to this day.

This brings up an important point about the impact that the loss of a child or spouse has on a family. While struggling with my own intense mourning, it was critical that I also fulfill my role as a mom to Ashley and Nathan who were both working through their own devastating loss. Often, the overwhelming grief felt by a parent will impact what they are able to give others, including their children or spouse. The way a parent mourns a child's or a spouse's death can have long-term repercussions for others in the family. This means finding a balance between times for shared grief and private grief while maintaining a confident and loving presence in the continuing life of the family.

Grief also elicits physical symptoms: headaches, digestive problems, fatigue, shakiness, tightness in your chest, erratic sleep, and a poor appetite or overeating. Grief is exhausting and these reactions are normal for a period of time as you grasp the magnitude of your loss.

A person may be tempted to desensitize the pain through alcohol, drugs, excessive television, busyness, or other coping mechanisms. Sadly, giving in to these temptations does hinder a person's ability to grieve in a healthy way. A quote from Sittser puts this into perspective:

> Many people form addictions after they experience loss. Loss disrupts and destroys the orderliness and familiarity of their world. They feel such desperation and disorientation in the face of this obliteration of order that they go berserk on binges. They saturate their senses with anything that will satisfy them in the moment because they cannot bear to think about the long-term consequences of loss.[35]

Phase Three: Despair

The third phase of grief is despair. This occurs when a person may have difficulty functioning in certain aspects of life. Depression and grief are inextricably linked and share many of the same characteristics including sadness, fatigue, anguish, apathy, negativity, hopelessness, and inability to concentrate. Depression can be exhausting, resulting in little energy available for normal functioning. Emotions vary, and at times we may feel pain and weep, and then at other times we may feel detached and without emotion.

For most individuals, this can be described as situational depression and it will subside over time. In contrast to clinical depression, situational depression from grief does not last as long, is not as intense, and does not immobilize you. However, if depression lasts and you have persistent feelings of hopelessness with no possibility of a better future, or if you are unable to cope with everyday tasks, it may indicate clinical depression. This needs to be treated by a counselor or physician. Depression may have a physiological component for which medication is appropriate.

Trusting God does not necessarily mean that you experience less grief. Nancy Guthrie, who suffered the loss of two infant children, shared a conversation with her husband where he expressed that he thought his faith would result in feeling less pain. "Our faith keeps us from being swallowed by despair. But I don't think it makes our loss hurt any less."[36]

My experience was similar. The knowledge that Danielle was in Heaven did not eliminate the pain, but it did put it into perspective. I grieved, but not with the disconsolate grief of those who have no hope of eternal life in Heaven.

Some people may feel they need to stay positive about their pain all of the time. Yet, consider David, a man after God's own heart, who shared his true feelings with God. "How long, LORD? Will you forget me forever? How long will you hide your face from me? How long must I wrestle with my thoughts and day after day have sorrow in my heart? How long will my enemy triumph over me?" (Psalm 13:1-2)

David is open and very frank with God, pleading for an answer. Yet, ultimately in verses 5 and 6, he realizes that he can continue to put his hope in God. "But I trust in your unfailing love; my heart rejoices in your salvation. I will sing to the LORD, for he has been good to me." (Psalm 13:5-6)

A person in the grieving process should not be rushed by others, because feelings and emotions need to be fully processed. Nonetheless, to proceed with healing, there will come a time when you have to say, "It is time to move on." You may resist this because it is often easier to give in to self-pity and other negative emotions rather than start moving back into life. There can be a temptation to wallow in grief.

I'm not suggesting that we deny our feelings to appear recovered. However, we must resist any tendency to settle into a mindset or way of living that identifies us permanently as a "grieving parent" or "grieving spouse." If you are struggling to shake off feelings of depression and feel like you've been in the despair phase for a significant amount of time, ask yourself what would help you to reinvest in life? You have a *choice* in your recovery. If you feel stuck in this phase, you may need to seek professional help because depression can be debilitating.

A grieving heart will start to feel stronger and you can experience joy again. Taking our heart-cries to God and reading the promises of His Word is the source of true hope and joy. God will not let us down. We can believe these words of Jesus in John 16:20: "Very truly I tell you, you will weep and mourn while the world rejoices. You will grieve, but your grief will turn to joy."

In Job 7:7, even this faith-filled man initially expresses the feeling that he will never again experience happiness. He cries, "Remember, O God, that my life is but a breath; my eyes will never see happiness again." Job thought he would "never see happiness again," but when we read the end of the book of Job, we find that God had something truly wonderful in store for him.

One evening as I wrestled with disturbing thoughts, I starting flipping through some index cards that Danielle had written verses on. One of the cards had Matthew 11:28-29 written on it: "Come to me, all you who are weary and burdened, and I will give you rest. Take my yoke upon you and learn from me, for I am gentle and humble in heart, and you will find rest for your souls."

As I read that verse over and over, I found myself calming down. I finally realized it as a personal request from Jesus asking me to hand my burdens over to Him so He could give me relief. What a gift we have to know that God speaks to us so personally through the Bible!

God states in His Word that He hears our cries and promises to comfort us. Psalm 10:17 states this promise, "You, LORD, hear the desire of the afflicted; you encourage them, and you listen to their cry." In Psalm 121:1-2 King David wrote, "I lift my eyes to the mountain, from where does my help come? My help comes from the Lord, maker of heaven and earth." Our true help in times of despair comes from God.

People suffering from intense grief may also experience a lost sense of self. They may feel, not only a loss of meaning and purpose, but may even wish to die. If you experience this thought, it is crucial that you seek help immediately. You may feel hopeless and life just doesn't seem worth living, but one of the most destructive choices you could consider as you deal with grief is suicide. Your life is so precious to God, even if you don't feel it. Your motivation may be to end the pain, but you will inflict a much greater pain on those you leave behind.

Phase Four: Healing and Renewal

The final phase of grief is healing and renewal. This is when I learned I could live a meaningful life without Danielle. It is an energizing time of shifting to a world with new possibilities and hope. Experiencing healing does not mean betraying memories or sentiments of the past. Healing and renewal are about acknowledging you have a new "normal" and accepting that things won't be the same again. This choice to let go of the past and move forward is usually a difficult transition. For most people, a number of changes and adjustments are made for new life to grow. Learning new skills and roles is the beginning.

Another change is in the way we think about our loved one. In the initial phases of grief, most of our thoughts are filled with loss and pain. Eventually those painful memories will be replaced by memories filled with joy and happier times that become a source of comfort.

In the first three phases, grief is more of a process of reacting to loss as one learns to manage a range of difficult feelings. As the grief journey continues to unfold, however, the grieving transitions into a more reflective process and includes a search for meaning.

During this time, my "Why?" questions were replaced by "How?" questions. "How can I adjust to life without Danielle?" "How can I become more Christ-like through this experience?" "How can I find new meaning and purpose?" This is a critical time of opportunity because a significant loss will never leave us the same.

As I moved into this phase, I was able, once again, to experience joy and look forward to life. A piece of my heart was taken when Danielle went home and the sadness may never disappear completely. But over time, the intensity of the pain decreases. As I came to accept what happened and understood that I could still live a fulfilled life, God gradually revealed a plan for my life. My personal healing was helped by reinvesting energy into a ministry involving Danielle's legacy. Our God, who makes all things new, wants to give you the grace to enjoy life again too.

I pray that as you go through your journey, you keep you eyes on the final destination, and realize Jesus is waiting for you at the finish line. Until that time, please remember you are inconceivably loved and God will never, ever leave you.

Grief's Natural Ebb and Flow Towards Joy

As mentioned earlier, people will move back and forth among these phases. There were many days when I felt like I was doing well when suddenly, something would trigger waves of fresh emotion. I felt like David in Psalm 42 where he asks God, "Why have you forsaken me?" Thankfully, I have also experienced calming truth on the heels of those unbearable moments. Like David concluded later in that Psalm, "I will put my hope in God! I will praise him again."

As I read the account of Jesus' suffering in Matthew 26, I see how He experienced aspects of the grief spiral. I cannot fathom the depth of the horrors that Jesus experienced in the Garden of Gethsemane. He knew he would be required to suffer at the hands of a vicious, vile and cruel enemy. As He contemplated the cross, Jesus experienced the intensity of what it would mean to willingly die and to have His own Father abandon Him. His anguish and despair is described in verses 37 and 38, "He took Peter and the two sons of Zebedee along with him, and he began to be sorrowful and troubled. Then he said to them, 'My soul is overwhelmed with sorrow to the point of death. Stay here and keep watch with me.'"

In verse 39, Jesus displayed His extreme distress, yet moved to the acceptance of His fate knowing that it was God's will and keeping the eternal purpose in focus. "Going a little farther, he fell with his face to the ground and prayed, 'My Father, if it is possible, may this cup be taken from me. Yet not as I will, but as you will.'" Jesus honestly expressed His soul's deepest despair, yet moved from that tormented feeling to a declaration of His faith. He trusted in God's love and power to reveal beautiful, eternal fruit out of His suffering—that fruit was the salvation of souls.

A Prayer For You

As I close this book, I can't tell you how important prayer was in my healing—prayer for myself and prayer from others. Prayer invites the presence of God into your pain and releases the power of His Holy Spirit to work in your heart and heal your sorrow. Prayer keeps the lines of communication open with the Lord, Who is your greatest source of comfort in your difficult time.

No special words or skills are necessary to pray. God knows how to interpret the groanings of our souls better than we do ourselves. But He wants us to embrace and engage Him. He waits patiently for us to reach out, then He rushes in with all compassion, power, and perfect love to bring mercy and beauty out of our agony!

Grab hold of God's invitation to ask Him for help. And ask others to pray for you. Whether angry, encouraged, hurting, or hopeful, tell God what you feel and need. He will meet you there.

I'm hoping this verse and prayer by Charles Swindoll, called *Courage for the Discouraged,* will help you draw near to God for comfort.

I waited patiently for the LORD; he turned to me and heard my cry. He lifted me out of the slimy pit, out of the mud and mire; He set my feet on a rock and gave me a firm place to stand. Psalm 40:1—2

Lord, we pray that You would bring relief when we are swamped with the ever-rising tide of discouragement. Encourage our hearts as we face those depressing, dark moments that leave us feeling hopeless and believing the lie that things will never change. Father, give us hope beyond the heartbreaks we experience. We cling to the inspired words of the apostle Peter that if we humble ourselves before the mighty hand of God, You will lift us up. You will exalt us at the proper time.

In humbleness, Father, we call upon You as Your children. We ask You to lift our spirits by transforming our minds. Strengthen us to see the value of dwelling on things that are true, honest, just, pure, lovely, and of good report. Help us to fix our mind on heavenly things rather than on those earthly things that drag us down.

Give us a rallying point around Your grace, dear Lord. We need that point of focus, our times being as they are and our moods so given to change. Thank You that Christ loves us and keeps on loving us. Thank You that while we were yet sinners, Christ died for us. Thank You that the grace that saved us keeps us saved, regardless of our doubts and other feelings.[37]

In Jesus great name I pray. Amen

ENDNOTES

Chapter 2

1.   Excerpt from Deadline by Randy Alcorn. Copyright © 2009 by Eternal Perspective Ministries. Used by permission of WaterBrook Multnomah, an imprint of the Crown Publishing Group, a division of Random House LLC. All rights reserved.

Chapter 4

2.   Taken from *A Grace Disguised* by Jerry Sittser. Copyright © 2004 by Gerald L. Sittser. Use by permission of Zondervan.

3.   Taken from *Heaven* by Randy Alcorn. Copyright © 2004 by Randy Alcorn. Used by permission of Tyndale House Publishers, Inc. All rights reserved.

4.   Ann Hibbard, *Shadows and Shining Lights* (Pomona, CA: Focus on the Family Publishing, 1990).

Chapter 5

5.   Taken from *If God is Good: Faith in the Midst of Suffering and Evil* by Randy Alcorn, Copyright © 2009 by Eternal Perspective Ministries. Used by permission of WaterBrook Multnomah, an imprint of the Crown Publishing Group, a division of Random House LLC. All rights reserved.

Chapter 6

6.   Taken from *When I Lay My Isaac Down* by Carol Kent. Copyright © 2004 by Carol Kent. Used by Permission of NavPress, All Rights Reserved.

7. Reprinted by permission. *A New Kind of Normal* by Carol Kent, Copyright © 2007, Thomas Nelson Inc. Nashville, Tennessee. All rights reserved.

8. Taken from *If God is Good: Faith in the Midst of Suffering and Evil* by Randy Alcorn, Copyright © 2009 by Eternal Perspective Ministries. Used by permission of WaterBrook Multnomah, an imprint of the Crown Publishing Group, a division of Random House LLC. All rights reserved.

9. Taken from *A Lifetime of Walking with Jesus* by Joni Eareckson Tada. Copyright © 2003 by Joni Eareckson Tada. Use by permission of Zondervan.

10. Used by permission of Lisa Jamieson, author of *Finding Glory in the Thorns.*

11. Taken from *If God is Good: Faith in the Midst of Suffering and Evil* by Randy Alcorn, Copyright © 2009 by Eternal Perspective Ministries. Used by permission of WaterBrook Multnomah, an imprint of the Crown Publishing Group, a division of Random House LLC. All rights reserved.

Chapter 7

12. Taken from *If God is Good: Faith in the Midst of Suffering and Evil* by Randy Alcorn, Copyright © 2009 by Eternal Perspective Ministries. Used by permission of WaterBrook Multnomah, an imprint of the Crown Publishing Group, a division of Random House LLC. All rights reserved.

13. Taken from *When God Weeps* by Joni Eareckson Tada and Steven Estes. Copyright © 1997 by Joni Eareckson Tada and Steven Estes. Use by permission of Zondervan.

14. Lewis, C.S., *The Chronicles of Narnia—The Last Battle* (NY: Scholastic, Inc., 1956). 211.

Chapter 10

15. Randy Alcorn, *Tell Me About Heaven* (Wheaton, Illinois: Crossway Books, 2007).

Chapter 11

16.   Taken from *When God Weeps* by Joni Eareckson Tada and Steven Estes. Copyright © 1997 by Joni Eareckson Tada and Steven Estes. Use by permission of Zondervan.

17.   Taken from *If God is Good: Faith in the Midst of Suffering and Evil by Randy Alcorn*, Copyright © 2009 by Eternal Perspective Ministries. Used by permission of WaterBrook Multnomah, an imprint of the Crown Publishing Group, a division of Random House LLC. All rights reserved.

18.   Beth Moore, *Daniel: Lives of Integrity, Words Of Prophecy*, (Nashville, TN: LifeWay Press, 2006). 66.

Chapter 12

19.   Taken from *Change Your Brain Change Your Life: The Breakthrough Program for Conquering Anxiety, Depression, Obsessiveness, Anger, and Impulsiveness* by Daniel Amen. Copyright © 1998 by Daniel Amen. Used by Permission of Random House, Inc. All Righs Reserved.

20.   Taken from *When God Weeps* by Joni Eareckson Tada and Steven Estes. Copyright © 1997 by Joni Eareckson Tada and Steven Estes. Use by permission of Zondervan.

21.   Evelyn Christianson, *Lord Change Me* (Colorado Springs, Colorado: Cook Communications, 1993). 186.

22.   By Charles R. Swindoll. Copyright © 1981, 2012 by Charles R. Swindoll, Inc. All rights are reserved worldwide.

23.   Taken from *Shattered Dreams* by Dr. Larry Crabb. Copyright © 1998 by Larry Crabb. Used by Permission of Random House, Inc. All Righs Reserved.

24.   Taken from *When God Weeps* by Joni Eareckson Tada and Steven Estes. Copyright © 1997 by Joni Eareckson Tada and Steven Estes. Use by permission of Zondervan.

Chapter 13

25.   Taken from *Choosing to See: A Journey of Struggle and Hope* by Mary Beth Chapman. Copyright © 2010 by Mary Beth Chapman. Use by permission of Baker Publishng.

Chapter 14

26. Taken from *A Grace Disguised* by Jerry Sittser. Copyright ©
     2004 by Gerald L. Sittser. Use by permission of Zondervan.
27. Reprinted by permission. *Get out of that Pit*, Beth Moore,
     Copyright © 2007, Thomas Nelson Inc. Nashville, Tennesse.
     All rights reserved.

Appendix—Advancing Toward Joy

28. C.M. Parkes, *Bereavement: Studies of Grief in Adult Life*
     (3rd ed.) (Philadelphia: Taylor & Francis, 2001).
29. C. Sanders, *Grief, The Mourning After: Dealing With Adult
     Bereavement* (2nd ed.). New York: John Wiley. 1999).
30. Taken From *Treatment of Complicated Mourning* by
     T.A.Rando. Copyright © 1993. Use by permission of
     Research Press, Champaign, IL.
31. Wright, H. Norman, *Recovering from the Losses of Life*,
     Revell, a division of Baker Publishing Group, 1993. Used by
     permission.
32. Taken from *A Grace Disguised* by Jerry Sittser. Copyright ©
     2004 by Gerald L. Sittser. Use by permission of Zondervan.
33. Kuenning, Delores, *Helping People through Grief*, Bethany
     House Publishers, 1987. Used by permission.
34. Wright, H. Norman, *Recovering from the Losses of Life*,
     Revell, a division of Baker Publishing Group, 1993. Used by
     permission.
35. Taken from *A Grace Disguised* by Jerry Sittser. Copyright ©
     2004 by Gerald L. Sittser. Use by permission of Zondervan.
36. Taken from *Holding On to Hope* by Nancy Guthrie. Copyright
     © 2002 by Nancy Guthrie. Used by permission of Tyndale
     House Publishers, Inc. All rights reserved.
37. Excerpt from Charles R. Swindoll, *The Prayers of Charles
     R. Swindoll Volume 1* (Plano:IFL Publishing House, 2010),
     12. Copyright © 2010 by Charles R. Swindoll, Inc. All rights
     are reserved worldwide. Used by permission.